MY LIFE IN CHRIST BEGAN AT FORTY

By
AVRIL ENGLISH

2 Corinthians 5:17 NIV Therefore, if anyone is in Christ, the new creation has come: The old has gone, the new is here!

My Life In Christ Began At Forty

Author: Avril English

Copyright © 2025 Avril English

The right of Avril English to be identified as author of this work has been asserted by the author in accordance with section 77 and 78 of the Copyright, Designs and Patents Act 1988.

First Published in 2025

ISBN 978-1-83538-705-4 (Paperback)
978-1-83538-707-8 (Hardback)
978-1-83538-706-1 (E-Book)

Book Cover Design and Layout by:
Maple Publishers
www.maplepublishers.com

Published by:
Maple Publishers
Fairbourne Drive, Atterbury,
Milton Keynes,
MK10 9RG, UK
www.maplepublishers.com

A CIP catalogue record for this title is available from the British Library.
All rights reserved. No part of this book may be reproduced or translated by any form or by any means, electronic or mechanical, including photocopying, recording or by any information storage and retrieval system without written permission from the author.
The views expressed in this work are solely those of the author and do not necessarily reflect the views of the publisher, and the publisher hereby disclaims any responsibility for them.

CONTENTS

Chapter 1 – The Beginning 5

Chapter 2 – Marriage 7

Chapter 3 – Separation 9

Chapter 4 – Second Marriage 12

Chapter 5 – Honeymoon 16

Chapter 6 – New Friends 17

Chapter 7 – Heartbreak 19

Chapter 8 – Stray Dog 23

Chapter 9 – Miscarriages 25

Chapter 10 – Pure Joy 27

Chapter 11 – Complications 29

Chapter 12 – Near Death 32

Chapter 13 – Born Again 34

Chapter 14 – God's Calling 39

Chapter 15 – Baptised 41

Chapter 16 – God's Promise 45

Chapter 17 – Conversion 47

Chapter 18 – Mum's Death 50

Chapter 19 – I Will Restore 54

Chapter 20 – Dad's Death 56

Chapter 21 – A Dream 61

Chapter 22 – Life Continues 63

Chapter 23 – Confidence in Christ 65

Chapter 24 – Negativity 67

Chapter 25 – Back to Work 69
Chapter 26 – My Adoptive Parents 72
Chapter 27 – God's Kingdom 74
Chapter 28 – The Enemy 77
Chapter 29 – New Car 81
Chapter 30 – Adoptive Dad Moves Away 83
Chapter 31 – New House 86
Chapter 32 – Driving Lessons 89
Chapter 33 – Moving Again 90
Chapter 34 – Marriage Proposal 94
Chapter 35 – A House of Prayer 97
Chapter 36 – A Miracle of God 99
Chapter 37 – Sent to Switzerland 101
Chapter 38 – Abandon 104
Chapter 39 – Benalmadena 110
Chapter 40 – Ruby Wedding 112
Chapter 41 – Gone Before Us 115
Chapter 42 – Leave the Land 118
Chapter 43 – Emergency 122
Chapter 44 – Clinical Summary 124
Chapter 45 – Settling Down 129
Chapter 46 – Conclusion 134
Chapter 47 – Acknowledgments 137

Chapter 1

The Beginning

I was born in Reading, Berkshire, on the 17th of April 1948 on a Saturday afternoon. Thunder rumbled and lightning struck as I entered into the world. I was Dad and Mum's fourth child. I had two older sisters and an older brother.

We lived in Reading for a while after my birth, but I was still a baby when we got the news that Dad was being moved to a new location to work in Stockton-On-Tees in County Durham. So, Mum began to pack up the house ready for the removal people to come and move us to our new location.

My older siblings were enrolled into the school at Stockton. They did not like the school, nor did they like the children where we were living. The local children were quite cruel towards them because they thought the way my siblings spoke was too posh for them.

My siblings were therefore really pleased when they learnt from our parents that Dad was given a new job and we were going to move to new development in a town called Newton Aycliffe, near Darlington.

Dad was a civil engineer, and he was chosen to be head engineer in this new development. We were going to live in a three-bedroom brand-new council house where there were only sixteen houses in the corner. We were allocated house number eight. It was a lovely house and on a corner plot.

We moved into our new home, and Dad and Mum had enough time to get the house in order before her new baby was to arrive. In the beginning of April, Mum gave birth to a baby boy to the delight of my elder brother who had wanted a baby brother for so long. Now his wish had come true.

We all settled into our new home and all of us were happy. We began to get to know the other families who lived in the corner and all the families seemed to get on well together. My young brother had the most adorable blonde curly hair, and my siblings and parents spoilt him rotten.

Unfortunately, I loved him, but I also was jealous of him as he took my place of being the youngest sibling in the family.

Life continued on and we were growing up nicely as a family. We were all very close and did a lot of things together.

My elder sister left school with good qualifications. She was going to go to college in Ambleside in the Lake District to train to be a teacher. My elder brother wanted to be an electrician, so he got employment with the Electricity Board. My other sister wanted to be a confectioner and got a job at Binns Bakery in Darlington. I never got asked what I would like to do for work. I was told to go and work in a supermarket, which I absolutely hated. My younger brother was offered a job at STC Telephone Communications. So, all in all, my siblings knew what they wanted to do, but me? I never felt adequate to do anything at all as I did not have any qualifications whatsoever. I did a number of different jobs but never felt happy or contented in any of them. I just plodded on.

I did work in Switzerland for ten months but the job I had was not very good. I was homesick and so I decided to return home to England. I did not want to live and work in Newton Aycliffe any longer, so when my dad's job changed again, moving him down to Basingstoke in Hampshire, I decided to move along with Dad and Mum.

Dad was on site working at his job, we were waiting for a house to become available for us to move into. In the meantime, I looked for a job and found one in Basingstoke as a cashier in a garage. Mum settled into our home and my sister came home from Switzerland and got a job at Marks & Spencer's.

Chapter 2
Marriage

We settled in Basingstoke. My sister was engaged to her boyfriend whom she had met whilst working in Switzerland. They were to be married in Switzerland in April 1973, at the English church in Zurich. My elder sister and I were asked to be her bridesmaids.

In the meantime, I was approached by my old boss from the garage, asking me to come back and work for the company. He offered me a better role with better conditions within the company. I was at this time engaged, and so I took into consideration how this role would be beneficial to me when I was married. I decided to accept the position, gave my notice to my employer and set a date to begin my new role.

I had my sister's wedding and my own wedding to plan. My fiancé and I were to be married six months after my sister. We were going to be married at St Michael's Church in Basingstoke. We arranged to rent accommodation for the first months of marriage, until our married quarter became available. My husband-to-be was in the RAF at Odiham in Hampshire we were able to have accommodation through them.

My family and I went to Switzerland to my sister's wedding, and we all had a lovely time. We spent a number of days there after the wedding then it was time for us to come home.

It was nearing the time I was to be married. Everything was in place for the wedding to take place in October.

The morning of my wedding was here, and I began to have reservations about whether I should get married or not. I felt I could not back out of the marriage, because I would let my parents and husband-to-be down, plus everything for the wedding had been arranged and booked and paid for. So, I felt I had to keep the promise I had made, regardless of how I was feeling.

This was the biggest mistake I have ever made. I was to find out a few months later the consequences of my actions.

I was so naïve when I married my husband at the age of twenty-five. I had been living in a fantasy world. I had read too many Mills & Boon novels.

I expected my husband to be like the characters within the books I had read, and he was not like any of them. He was very cold towards me and did not show me the love and affection I was expecting as a young married woman. My marriage was cold and loveless.

I continued to try and make the marriage work. But I spent most nights in the other room crying my eyes out because I felt so unloved. I had always believed in marriage and had saved myself for twenty-five years, because I believed in saving yourself for the man you married, and that marriage was for life.

I continued with daily life, coming and going from work. A colleague at work began to flirt with me and show me the attention I craved but never received from my husband. When I first met this man, I did not even like him. He was married and he was not my type at all. Even though I knew all this I lapped up the attention he gave to me and even though we both were married this did not seem to matter.

Things began to change, especially when the colleagues and I went out for our Christmas do. This man made a play for me, and he kissed me under the mistletoe. I now found myself getting into something even deeper which I felt I had no control over. When we worked on shift together, he would flirt with me, and I would flirt with him. This seemed to be exciting for me. I knew in my heart what I was doing was absolutely wrong, especially knowing he had a wife at home, but this did not seem to deter me. My principles had gone out of the window. I liked the attention this man was giving me as I did not get the attention at home. I cannot make any kind of excuse for what I was doing, but all I can say is I paid the price for my behaviour.

Eventually I came to the place in my life where I knew I had to separate from my husband. I had made a pact with my colleague that I would separate from my husband, and he told me he would separate from his wife.

Chapter 3

Separation

Things were about to become even worse for me. I had separated from my husband and went back home to live with my parents. We had to give up our married quarter because of the separation. My husband had moved back onto the camp, and it was time for us to sort out the married quarter.

My Mum came with me to pack up my things. I had to put the things I was taking from the marital home into storage.

While we were packing, my husband announced out of the blue that he was going to give the lawnmower to his friend as a present. I thought at the time how odd his words were. When giving something to a friend of yours you would say, 'I am giving my mate the lawnmower', not 'giving it to him as a present'. My alarm bells began to ring. In the moment he spoke those words to me, everything in our marriage fell into place. He was in love with his friend and always had been. It had taken me seventeen months to find out this truth.

On the way home Mum and I discussed the statement that my husband had made. Up until that point I had kept everything about my marriage and what was happening between my husband and myself between us. I had not talked about what was going on within my marriage with anyone, not even the man I was going out with. I did not want anyone to know what I had been going through with him or about the man I was seeing on the side. I had kept everything that had been going on in my life to myself. Unbeknownst to me, this was making me ill.

Now, everything had come out regarding my husband. I told Mum everything that went on within our marriage and she could not believe what had happened to me. I had yet to tell my parents what was going on with my married friend.

When eventually I got around to telling my parents that I was going out with a married man, as you can imagine they were none too pleased with my behaviour. However, by this time, with everything that had been happening to me I was on the verge of a breakdown. I had been prescribed nerve tablets by my doctor, and one night I was so low that I decided I didn't want to be here anymore, so I planned to take tablets to end my life.

I began to take them when something within me stopped me. I had no idea what was going on, but I stopped there and then and did not take any more. My elder sister told my parents to leave me alone as she could see I was not in a good place, so they did. Dad had been around to the married man's flat and challenged him. This made no difference to me as I was still working with him, and he had a hold upon me. I could not see a way out of my situation.

Then one day I saw an advertisement for a job which I applied for at AWRE Aldermaston. I talked it through with my parents and decided that I would apply for a position there. I got a letter to say I had an interview, so the ball was rolling. At the time I did not tell my colleague what I was about to do. I thought I would wait to see if I got the position I had applied for.

All these things were happening to me when my parents dropped the bombshell that they were looking to move to the north of England to be near my elder sister.

I now had the added pressure that soon I would no longer have a place to live. My parents asked me to move with them, but because I was going through a divorce and changing my job, I felt that I did not want to go with them.

So, now I had to find somewhere to live. If I got a job at Aldermaston, then accommodation would be available to me in the hostel but, as yet, I still was waiting to hear whether I had been successful in my interview. So, my life was hanging in the balance, and I had no idea which way to go. I felt so alone. I told one of the girls whom I worked with that my parents were moving, and she offered me a room at her place with her husband and children. So, I jumped at the chance and took the room.

But I had made a mistake going there. They did not allow me to use the facilities I needed to get washed or cook or do my washing, so it was not working out for me.

Mum and Dad had moved by this time. I had no idea what I could do. This is when my friend from work suggested we find a place and live together. I took him up on his suggestion and he found us a flat to live in above a parade of shops where we were able to go to work.

I retrieved the furniture I had put into storage and thought it would be nice to have some of my things around me. I tried to make a home for us, but it was not working out as he did not get his own way, and his wife was putting demands upon him by sending him all the household bills.

The man I was with was becoming more unbearable. He found fault with everything I was doing. He was becoming more aggressive and abusive with his drinking. I was so pleased when I received a letter from AWRE offering me the position at Aldermaston. I immediately thought to myself this is the way out I had been looking for. I accepted the position and had a start date.

A very close friend and her husband helped me beyond measure. I had told them what had been going on. They had been at my wedding, so they knew some of the difficulties I had been through with my husband but had no idea what I had got myself into now. My friend and her husband suggested I put all my things back into storage. They said I could live with them until the room became available at the hostel.

We arranged for the storage company to come and collect my belongings when he was at work, and I knew he would not be around. My friend and I packed everything as quickly as we could. We had never packed anything so fast in our lives.

Finally, it was done, the storage company left, and I got the flat key and put it through the front door, and my friend and I left to go to her house.

Everything had been arranged for me to begin my new job. I had arranged for the site bus to pick me up and drop me off at the end of their road. I did this until a room had become available for me to move into at the hostel.

I was with my friends for two weeks. My friend's husband took me to the hostel and settled me in and we said we would keep in touch. I had a key to my own room, and this helped me feel secure.

I began my job and found the people I was working with to be kind. I began to settle in. I was still very nervous having left such a stressful situation behind me; I couldn't help but keep looking around to see if my ex-boyfriend was behind me.

I did not want anyone within the hostel to know that I was married. I met some northern girls who had invited me to go for a drink at the bar at the hostel. I went with them but did not give them any information about what had happened to me or that I was married. They were nice people, and I seemed to get on well with them. They worked on site as well, so at least I was making friends within the hostel. The hostel had activities going on nightly in the bar for the employees. So, my life carried on. I had my breakfast and evening meals in the hostel and was able to lunch on site, so things were working out for me at last.

Chapter 4
Second Marriage

I met my second husband in the hostel at Tadley. We were sitting down one Sunday lunchtime having dinner and we seemed to get on well together. He worked for the MOD Police. I was having a Sunday lunch and was eating one of the roast potatoes when my tooth broke. I told him what had happened. He told me to make a dentist appointment and that he would come with me to the appointment. This was the beginning of our friendship.

We talked a lot. He told me that he was separated from his wife and three children. He did not go into great detail at the time about what happened between them but he was unable to have the children with him because he was in the police force and his children lived in Bognor Regis with his wife, who still lived in their marital home with her new boyfriend.

This really made me sit up and listen. I know I had a rough time with my husband and man friend, but this man had had it worse than I did. He had lost his home and three children... how hard that must have been for him. If I had been feeling sorry for myself before, this made me sit up and not feel sorry for myself any longer. His circumstances were far worse than mine ever could be.

We began to date and began to fall for one another. He was very caring towards me. I told him a bit about what had happened to me. I had only been on one date with him when he was talking about being able to get married quarters. We decided that we would get our divorces and get married as soon as our divorces came through. We were using the same solicitor. I was going to divorce my husband for 'unreasonable behaviour'. My boyfriend was going to allow his wife to divorce him even though he had the grounds for a divorce. He did not want his children to think badly about their mum, even though she was living with the man she had left him for. Our solicitor tried to persuade him to do otherwise but he was quite adamant he would allow her to divorce him on grounds that he had committed adultery with a friend of hers. He hadn't done this for her but for his children as he did not want his children to think badly of their mother. His wife had made a pact with her husband that they would not tell the children anything of what truly happened between them in their marriage. Even though she was living with the man she had left her husband for. So, being the man he is, he never divulged to his children truly what had happened between them.

After this, around Christmas time, my husband-to-be was missing his children terribly. He said he wanted to finish things between us. I was absolutely devastated. He told me this just as he left for nightshift. I just could not get my head and heart around this, as I thought things were going really well between us. He told his police friends that he had finished his relationship with me. I did not know one of his so-called friends kept making passes at me and he wanted to go out with me. I did not want him, nor did I want to go out with him. That night when I was alone in bed, and he was at work I cried and cried until I could cry no more. I did not understand why I was being treated like this. I had had it with my first husband and the man I had worked with, now he too was rejecting me. I did not know how much more I could take with relationships, they all seemed to go wrong. I believed in marriage and when I married my first husband, I thought it was 'until death do us part', but that did not work out the way I thought it would. My life seemed to be going down a dark spiral and I did not seem to be in control of anything, the more I tried the worse it became.

When my boyfriend had finished his night shift and was back at the hostel, he came back to his room, put his things away, then he knocked on my door. He wanted to talk things through with me. I listened to what he was saying, and he told me he couldn't cope with not being with his children at Christmas time and it was breaking his heart.

His wife had left him to be with a man who was nineteen years old, a man who was a lot younger than he was. This was hard for him to get his head around. He saw this man as too young to be involved with his children, yet he had no control over the situation. I could understand this, and at least now I knew the real reason he wanted to finish things with me. Everything was out in the open. It was not because he didn't love me, it was because of his children. We made up and things became stronger in our relationship.

We had planned to get married as soon as we were divorced from our partners. Our divorces came through in August 1977, and we were free to marry one another. The date had been set, we were to be married on 10 September 1977, at Newbury Registry Office.

His ex-wife also got married in August. They all moved away to Scotland where her husband was in the Navy.

I knew when we married, I would have to maintain his three children, and I accepted this. We were going to live in a police quarter near to where my husband worked.

I had arranged with the storage company to deliver to us the things I had put into storage with them. We prepared our home with the things that we had. Friends were so good to us; they gifted some things to us too.

We had decided to live in the small room as we did not have much furniture. We had the room fitted with carpet, put two chairs, a sideboard and a small television in the room and made it as homely as we could. We put curtains up and made it a base to live in until we could afford to get some furniture. We bought a second-hand twin tub washing machine and a cooker, so at least we could do our washing and were able to eat. The rest would come at a later date. We bought carpet for the bedroom floor, curtains for the window, and we had a bed to sleep in. We had the bare essentials to begin our married life. We would move into the house after the wedding.

The night before we were married, we had a combined celebration. It was my fiancé's birthday, so we celebrated with friends we had met in Boundary Hall and some of our colleagues we worked with.

One of my colleagues, whom I was friendly with, invited me to stay with her and her dad the night before I was to be married. She would take me to the registry office the next day. We had invited a man she spent time with doing crosswords with on her breaks at work. She liked him so we invited him to come along to our celebrations. They seemed to hit it off and he invited her out on a date. She had never been married before. He had been married before and had two grown up daughters.

It was a beautiful sunny day on the day of our wedding. My husband-to-be was waiting for me to arrive at Newbury Registry Office, with our witnesses. They were waiting for me to arrive with my friend. We were married at 12 o'clock on the 10th of September 1977.

Now I was married once again. I was really happy, happier than I had been in a long while. I really loved my husband and was proud to be his wife. We had bought a Triumph 1300 car before we married, and we left the registry office in it to go to the restaurant. We met our guests at the restaurant where we were going to have a three-course meal. We could not afford an elaborate wedding as we got married on our salaries. There were five people at our wedding, this included us. We booked the restaurant, and our guests could individually choose their meal from the menu. We all enjoyed the meal, and we celebrated our wedding day with them. Then it was time for us to leave. We were going on honeymoon to visit my husband's parents in Bognor Regis for the first week and to visit my parents in Newcastle-Upon-Tyne for the second week.

Chapter 5

Honeymoon

We were on our way to Bognor Regis, to spend our honeymoon with my husband's parents. We were driving up South Harting Hill when our car began to struggle to get up the hill. My husband was able to park the car in a safe place to stop the car and have a look at the engine to see what was going on. He told me he thought the engine had moved forward. He had to drive slowly to Bognor Regis and hopefully we would get there in one piece. He drove the car to a garage that his brother managed. When we arrived, his brother was waiting with the mechanics ready to look at the car. The mechanics came back with the news that the car was unrepairable.

We needed to buy another car on hire-purchase, so I rang Mum and Dad and asked them if they would they be guarantors for us.

My Dad said, "No."

I was in floods of tears. I had never asked my parents to do anything for me, and the first time I ask them to help me out, my dad refuses.

My Mum could tell I was in a bit of a state. We were on honeymoon, we did not expect this to happen to us, and now we were stuck in Bognor Regis. We were supposed to go to the north of England afterwards, but now because of what happened would not be able to go. When Mum came on the phone we talked, and she could see we needed help. She spoke to Dad, and he relented, and they agreed to be guarantors for us. My husband's parents were not in any position to help us as his dad sadly had liver cancer.

My parents agreed to be our guarantors, so we went ahead and bought a white Austin Maxi from my brother-in-law's garage. Everything was sorted out and now we could enjoy our time with my husband's family and my own family.

Chapter 6

New Friends

We began living our lives in a village, just five minutes away from my husband's work. I had arranged with the AWRE to get the site bus at the bus stop at the end of road where we lived. This is where I met my new friends. We all worked at the AWRE but in different departments, and we all lived fairly close to one another. Sometimes, we would meet up in our lunchbreaks and eat together. Life was settling down nicely for us, and I was getting into a daily routine. My husband did shift work and so we had to plan everything around his shifts.

My friend from the bus stop kept inviting me to go and meet his wife. They lived in one of the flats down the road from where we were living. I was getting to know him, and I still was very shy around others, but eventually I did go to his flat and meet his wife, and she was a great woman. We really hit it off with one another and we became close friends. I was able to talk everything through with her and knew I could trust her to keep the things we shared to herself and not gossip to others about me. These were two people who became very important in my life.

It took many years for us to get our home together. We were committed to supporting my husband's children and were paying maintenance monthly for their upkeep. The amount we had to pay took all of my wages, so we lived on my husband's wages. So, we could only do things bit by bit to get our home together. Child support was killing us, but I knew what I was taking on when I married him. Things were very tight financially.

My sister who lived in Switzerland came to stay with us for a holiday. She could not believe how we were living. I will never ever forget the love and generosity she showed us. As soon as she saw we had no carpets on the floor apart from the small room where we were living, she took the pocket money she had saved for her holiday and she spent it on us, providing us with a carpet for the lounge, hallway and landing. Because she covered this for us, we could afford a new three-piece suite on hire purchase, and as well as a second-hand table and four chairs, plus curtains for the lounge. I was truly grateful for the generosity of my sister. It was nice to have somewhere comfortable to sit down. Yes, it had taken us a while to do this, but we really appreciated what we had and everything my sister had done for us.

Chapter 7

Heartbreak

My life was in a crisis once again. I had not been married two years when I found my marriage was in trouble. I had been invited to go to Switzerland to stay with my sister and her husband. My husband was really encouraging me to go to Switzerland. He took me to Heathrow Airport to catch my flight to Switzerland, but at the airport he seemed distant. I shrugged it off thinking I was imagining things.

Whilst I was in Switzerland I had a dream. I dreamt my husband was with another woman and was having an affair with her. In the dream I could see this woman clearly. She was a policewoman he was working with. The next day I told my sister about the dream I'd had. She thought I was imagining things. I could not get the dream out of my head. When my husband rang me up, I could sense a division between us. I could not shake off the dream nor the way he was behaving towards me on the phone… there was just something in his tone of voice that made me uneasy, and I was unable to put my finger upon it. I decided I was going to go home earlier than anticipated. I got my flight booked and gave the details of my flight number to my husband and he would pick me up at Heathrow Airport.

My husband was at the airport to pick me up from my flight. He did not give me the warm welcome I had expected from him. He did not show any kind of affection towards me, and I was like a stranger to him. I just knew something was not right between us.

We were in the car and on our way home when I blurted out to him, "You're having an affair, aren't you?"

Of course he denied it. When we got home and indoors, I did not let it go, I wanted to get to the bottom of what was going on in our marriage and I dug my heels in. By the end of the night, he admitted to me he'd had an affair. He told me he went with someone he met in Bognor Regis, whilst visiting his Mum. I knew that the dream I'd had in Switzerland was the truth.

I thanked him for telling me the truth. I needed time to think things through. I knew it was the policewoman he was working with so I had to wait before I could say anything to him.

An opportunity came my way one morning while I was going to work. I was using the car to go to work as my husband had been on night shift and the car was available to me. I stopped off at the corner shop to get a paper to take to work. When I was coming out of the shop, I saw a policewoman coming towards me. This was the woman I had seen in my dream.

I blurted out to her, "Hello!" And I called her by her name. I continued on and asked her how she was. She looked shocked as she looked at me then looked at the car I was driving. I had taken her completely by surprise.

When she went to work that evening, she approached my husband at work and told him what had happened at the corner shop that morning. Now he knew that I knew who the person was that he was having the affair with. It was all out in the open now. My husband was unable to hide it any longer. I had already approached his Mum about the so-called affair he'd had in Bognor Regis. So, that had been ruled out immediately.

When he came home from night shift that morning I challenged him again, only this time he admitted that it was the policewoman and that he had fallen in love with her and out of love with me. I was absolutely devastated. I went to work but I was in such a state my boss sent me home. He told me to go to the doctors and get a sick note to give me time to sort this mess out.

Now I had first-hand experience of what it was like for a husband to have an affair with someone else. This time I was the wife. I now knew exactly how my ex-boyfriend's wife must have felt when he cheated on her with me. What do they say? 'What goes around comes around.' I had got the punishment I had deserved for what I had done to her.

My husband's affair had been going on for a number of months. This was one of the reasons my husband encouraged me to go to Switzerland as he wanted to be with her.

Now, I had to do something about this situation. I was not going to allow him or her to treat me this way. I had been faithful to him. I had supported him, his ex-wife, and their children but I was not going to support a mistress as well. He had turned my life upside down. Now it was time I had to do something about this.

When my husband was on the 2-10 pm shift, I phoned up Boundary Hall and booked him into a room. I packed his belongings and put them into a suitcase. When he came in from work, I told him he was not staying at home as I had booked him into a room at Boundary Hall. He did not put up a fight, I got his suitcase, put it into the car and then he got into the car with me, and I dropped him off at Boundary Hall.

As he got his suitcase out of the car, I said to him, "It's funny. We met here and now I am leaving you here."

I left him there and I cried all the way home. My husband had broken my heart. I loved him so much, but now I was an emotional wreck and the pedestal I had him on was destroyed for good.

It seemed I could not stay married for two years. It had happened in my first marriage, now it was happening again in my second marriage. I was heartbroken, as I still loved him, but felt I could not allow his behaviour to continue towards me. I thought something was wrong with me, but even though I thought this I was not going to allow this to happen to me any longer.

When I got home, I needed someone to talk to, so I phoned my elder sister, who lived in Newcastle-Upon-Tyne. I told her what had happened to me. She listened and told me she was going to have a word with Mum and ask her to come and stay with me to support me. She felt I should not be left alone and be on my own. We said our goodbyes as she left to make a phone call to Mum. After speaking to Mum, Mum phoned me and told me she would come the next day to stay with me.

I went to bed exhausted but found my mind was going round and round in circles over the things that had taken place.

While Mum was staying with me, I had arranged to see my husband. We arranged to meet at the police club. I thought he had taken the documents I needed to insure the car. When I met him, it was like meeting a complete stranger, not my husband. We talked about the insurance document I needed. He told me he did not seem to think he had the document.

We finished our drinks and went to his room. When we got their things spun out of control, we had the biggest row ever. All my pent-up anger, feelings and emotions I had stored up against him and his mistress came out. I let rip. I told him I was going to divorce him. I also said to him that if he thought I was going to support a wife, three children and now a mistress he was sadly mistaken. I was going to name his mistress in our divorce. I would notify the police about their relationship. I told him how they both had not considered me so now I would not consider them. They would have to take the consequences for what they had done to me. I was furious and very, very hurt. I could be hot-headed at times. I left him in floods of tears.

When I reached home, I said to my Mum, "Well I have really blown it this time. He will never come back now." I was in a worse state than I was before.

I had to go to work the next day, I was sure my colleagues would be able to see in my face the mess I was in. I had to go to the office and see my boss. He was very understanding towards me when I told him what had happened. He told me to go to the doctors to explain what had happened. I made the appointment and went and kept the appointment at the doctors.

The doctor said something very strange to me. "Avril, your husband must have loved you once. I suggest when he rings you again, ask him if he would go on holiday with you, to get some sunshine and get away from it all."

So, when he rang me, I did what the doctor had suggested. Much to my surprise my husband agreed, and said he would arrange a holiday for us. My doctor had given me a sick note, so I handed it to my boss and went on sick leave.

When I told Mum what I was going to do, she was not pleased with me. I made my decision, and I wanted to try and make our marriage work. After all it was my life. Mum decided to go home and so I took her to the train station to catch her train.

When I looked at how my husband had treated me, he always been good and kind towards me. He had a great sense of humour and even if I was down, he could always make me laugh. I took everything into consideration - how he had treated me from the moment we met, and I came to the conclusion I had to go on holiday and see if we could talk things through and try to make our marriage work. I had to take responsibility too for my part of our marriage and why it had broken down. I had faults like he had, and I accepted I was as much to blame as he was. I wanted to change and make our marriage work. I thought one mistake was not a good enough reason to allow our marriage to end in divorce, so I was willing to put my energy into my marriage and hopefully my husband did too. I would try and make it work as well.

My husband had booked for us to go to Amsterdam, for a long weekend, it was weekend of my husband's birthday and our second wedding anniversary, I did not want to be a hypocrite and buy cards and presents for him, so I just let it go. We had our holiday together, and although at times it was awkward, we were trying to make our marriage work.

Chapter 8
Stray Dog

A Labrador dog was roaming around the police main gate. My husband had phoned me at work to see how I felt about looking after the dog until he had found its owner. So, I agreed with him, as long as the dog had been checked out by the vet and was okay, we would look after her.

The vet said he thought the dog was about two years old and he thought she seemed to be in good health. We decided to keep her until someone came to claim her. We gave her a good bath as she was very dirty and smelly from wandering the streets. We gave her temporary accommodation until someone came to claim her.

We started to become attached to the dog, and when no one came to claim her, we decided we would keep her, and we named her Victoria. We bought Victoria all the creature comforts and gave her the best we could. Victoria was now a part of our family.

I really believed Victoria was sent to us to help us in our marriage. Now we had something else to focus on beside one another, our marriage seemed to be getting better.

Victoria got into all kinds of mischief whilst we were at work. One day my husband came home from work to find she had opened the freezer and had a pack of butter in her mouth. Goodness knows what else she had eaten. Another time my husband found her eating the contents of his lunch bag. She had eaten his backache pills, his shoe-polishing brushes, and other things inside his bag. She was absolutely fine and to be honest I found this quite funny. We were really enjoying ourselves with her. She brought so much joy and laughter into our lives; we were so pleased she was our dog.

We began to talk about having children as we had been married a number of years. This was going to be a bit difficult because when my husband was married to his first wife, he'd had a vasectomy due to her being told that having more children could be dangerous for her life.

We decided to go and talk to our doctor to see if it was possible to have his vasectomy reversed. The doctor told us it was possible to do this. The doctor was referring my husband to a consultant in Basingstoke.

The appointment arrived and we went to have the consultation. The consultant explained to us about the operation. He told us how the procedure would be done and continued to tell us the pros and cons of the operation and how successful the procedure would be. I also would have to be checked out to make sure I could have children. I had to go into hospital and have a 'laparoscopy', (keyhole surgery), to see if everything was okay within my womb. They checked me all out and everything seemed to be okay with me. So, we both decided if it enabled us to have a child then we would go ahead and try. The consultant arranged a date for my husband to have surgery.

We were waiting for the letter to come with the date he was to have his operation. We received an appointment for the operation, it was going to take place at Alton Hospital, in Hampshire. At the time I never realised how big this operation was going to be, if I had known what the operation entailed, I would have probably thought twice.

But he went through with it, and afterwards the consultant told him what he could and could not do. I made sure he did everything the consultant had told him to do. We would have to wait to see the result of the operation and whether it had been successful or not.

Chapter 9

Miscarriages

My husband began to recover from his operation. The consultant was pleased about how the operation had gone. For a while we had to wait before we could try to have a family, but finally we were given the all-clear. Now all we had to do was get pregnant.

I became pregnant a number of times but miscarried very early on in pregnancy. We never gave up though. As far as I was concerned, if we were meant to have a child, nothing would stop it. At least I was getting pregnant. After a number of miscarriages, I became pregnant again and this time I was given a due date for the baby.

We were so excited about our forthcoming child. What we did not expect was that I would go into labour in the eleventh week of pregnancy. The doctor was sent for, and he came out, examined me and told me what he wanted me to do. So, I did what was asked of me. After a number of days, my situation did not get any better and the doctor called an ambulance, I was going to be admitted into hospital.

On 7 March 1984 I lost the baby. I was absolutely devastated. I was very emotional with the pain of losing the child that I'd longed for. It was an experience I would never forget.

The hospital staff were very matter of fact about the death of my child. They did not show me any compassion or understanding about what I had been through. They did not ask me if I wanted to know the sex of the child, nor did they ask me if I wanted to see the child. It felt very cold and calculating. I was told I had to go to theatre to have a dilation and curettage (D&C), to clear the uterine lining after my miscarriage. I stayed in hospital for another day. They told me I was able to go home the next day.

Losing the baby had really hit me hard. It has taken me a long time to come to terms with my loss. My hormones were all over the place. I felt very empty and was grieving for the child I'd lost. I felt so alone and did not have anyone to confide in. My husband was unable to show any kind of emotion about the loss of our child. This could have been the effect of losing his other three children. The only thought that comforted me was that I got to eleven weeks in pregnancy this time. At least I kept this child longer than any other pregnancy I'd had.

In April, I was at home recovering from the loss of my baby, when there was a knock at the front door. When I opened the door, my husband's two boys were standing in front of me. They had come to find their dad. They had ridden their bicycles from where they were living in Reading to find him. I was amazed to know the boys had remembered where we lived. They looked older than the last time we'd seen them.

They were just about to say, 'You don't remember us?' When I said to them that, yes, I could see without a shadow of a doubt these were my husband's two boys!

When my husband came home from work, he couldn't believe his eyes, seeing his two boys in our home. The boys told their dad they had moved back into the area a number of months previously, but their mum had not informed my husband.

The two children did not want their Mum to know they were with him. My husband chatted to the boys for a little while. He told the boys he would put their bikes on the roof rack of our car and take them home. He did not want anything to happen to them especially as their Mum had no idea where they were. He promised them that he would speak to their mother.

After losing the baby, this was a kind of comfort for me my husband's children had come back into our lives.

In June I became pregnant again. I was told I must not do anything until I got over the dangerous period, this for me was sixteen weeks. The hospital was keeping a close eye on me. I kept having regular scans to make sure everything in the pregnancy was going well.

I was told after the sixteen weeks I could return to work. My friends were really excited for me. Although I was constantly being sick, the doctor told me this was a good sign that the pregnancy was good. I did not like being sick, but I was happy the pregnancy was going well.

I worked up until the time came for me to go onto maternity leave. I arranged a party with my colleagues, and it went well. My friends bought me a lot of gifts for our child, and I was so happy. I could not wait for our child to be born.

Chapter 10

Pure Joy

I managed to carry the pregnancy full term. I was preparing for the arrival of our baby. I bought the clothes and other essentials the baby would need. I washed all the clothes ready for when the child was born and prepared a suitcase to take into the hospital when my time came.

The day came when I went into labour. It was Friday 22 March. I was at my friend's hairdressers shop talking to my friends there. My husband was busy decorating the baby's room, at long last.

My friends and I were going to tease the owner of the hairdresser's shop. I had become very friendly with her and the girls that worked for her. I said to the girls that morning, 'When she comes in, tell her that I have had a baby girl this morning.' We all laughed as we thought it was funny. I left the hairdressers shop to go home.

In the afternoon I went back into the hairdressers shop to see my friend's face. She looked shocked when she saw me walking into her shop.

"I thought you were in hospital having a baby girl!" She said.

I just laughed. My friend was doing a client's hair whom I happened to know as well. We all laughed at the expression on her face. My friend had the last laugh though. I felt a trickle of water and knew something was happening within me. I told her I had better go straight home, as I felt the baby was on its way.

I left the shop and went home and told my husband what had happened. He told me to phone the hospital. After speaking to the hospital staff on the maternity ward, they told me to come into hospital straight away.

My husband's response to me was this, "You will have to wait until the coving has stuck on the wall."

This was because the adhesive was still tacky, then he could take me to the hospital.

I arrived at the hospital around four o'clock. The midwife assessed me and told me the waters behind the baby's head had broken. The midwife put a monitor on the baby's head to monitor the baby's heartbeat whilst I was in labour and put a monitor on me.

The labour was progressing nicely. My husband and I still had not chosen a baby's name. We had chosen one if the baby was a boy, but if it was a girl we did not have a name. So, whilst I was in labour the midwife, my husband and I were going through the alphabet and when we came to the letter "K" we chose a name for a baby girl. At that precise moment I found myself saying, "Come on 'K', and she was born into the world, the most beautiful baby girl I had ever seen. We had named her, and she weighed in at 6ibs 1oz. She came into the world at 23:37pm on Friday 22 March 1985.

When 'K' was born the midwife was concerned for me. She called for a doctor to come and see me as the placenta had not come away as it should. The doctor told the midwife the placenta had broken up after the birth, and it was in pieces. They did what they could at the time for me to get the placenta to come away.

They moved me to a side ward, where I could have peace and quiet. I had not slept since the delivery of our child. After two weeks the hospital discharged me from hospital, but I was told in no uncertain terms was I to leave my home.

My mum and my sister were going to be at Heathrow Airport to catch a flight back to Switzerland. The airport was a half hour away from me and so they phoned me and arranged for me and the baby to meet them there. I told them it was impossible for me to go to the airport, as the hospital told me I was not to leave home no matter what. Mum and my sister were not happy I was not going to the airport, but there was nothing I could do about it; I had to do what the hospital told me to do.

Chapter 11

Complications

On the Monday morning, I had been home from the hospital a couple of days when I went to the toilet and saw I was losing blood. My husband phoned the doctor immediately. The doctor told my husband the midwife was on her way. When she examined me, the midwife saw I was haemorrhaging. She phoned the doctor immediately, and he told her to give me an injection to control the bleeding, and to phone for an ambulance to take my daughter and I into hospital without delay. My husband was going to follow the ambulance in his car behind us.

My GP had informed the hospital, and the staff was waiting on the ward for my arrival. I was put into a side ward with the baby. When I got to the hospital the bleeding had stopped due to the injection the midwife had given to me. The doctor who examined me on the ward at my arrival told me there was no need to do the dilation and curettage (D&C) procedure, in which the cervix is dilated and a special instrument is used to scrape the uterine lining, because I had stopped bleeding. I insisted I have a D&C, and after some deliberation the doctors decided they would do the operation.

My husband and the nurses on the ward were going to take care of the baby whilst I was in theatre. I had expressed milk for the baby to give to her whilst I was in theatre. What I did not expect was how long I would be away from her. I was in theatre for three and half hours. The nurses had to give my baby bottled milk until I came back from theatre and into my room.

My husband and daughter were waiting for me in my room. In theatre they had to give me blood transfusions and put saline drips in my arm to give me antibiotics. My husband told me afterwards he had been really worried because of the length of time I was in theatre. I was able to chat to him for a while, but I could see he was tired and so was I, so I told him to go home and get some rest and see to the dog as she had been on her own for some time. My daughter was staying in the hospital with me because I was breast feeding her.

I asked my husband to bring me more clothes into the hospital for her. It was a good job I did. Because of the medication I was on and because I was breast feeding her the medication was going straight through her. We had to continually change her as she was reacting to my medication. We went through a lot of nappies and clothes.

The consultants the next day were doing their daily rounds. When they came to me, they apologized to me for what had happened in the theatre. They told me my womb was in such a mess after delivering my child. The placenta had not been expelled properly after the birth and it took the surgeons a long time to clean up the womb. They had trouble controlling the bleeding. This was why they had to give me blood transfusions and what kept me in theatre longer than they had expected.

Now, I understood fully why the doctors on the maternity ward told me not to leave home when they discharged me. They had expected me to haemorrhage. I could not blame anyone for the way things had turned out after the birth of my child. All I had to do was recover from the operation, then I could go home and get settled down with my child.

This was not the end of my time in hospital. I had to constantly go in and out of hospital, having D&Cs because there was still placenta left in the womb, this continued right up until October of 1985.

They found this out when I was having tests for another problem I had. They found out on one of the x-rays, on a kidney x-ray my womb was still open. Once again, they sent me down to theatre for a D&C and hopefully this time the problem would be resolved.

I also was under surgical consultants because of the pain I was having in my abdomen. So, I was under two departments, surgical and also gynaecology. Eventually, they sorted me out on gynaecology, then all I had to do was get sorted out in the surgical ward.

On top of this, my husband had an appointment at the Reading Hospital, he had a lump in his neck. The hospital wanted him to go into the hospital to have the lump removed immediately. The trouble was we were in different hospitals, and we had our daughter to consider. I phoned my Mum and asked her if she could come and help us out. Her response to me was, no, she would not come. I was devastated, how could she treat me this way when I was so desperate? At a drop of a hat Mum attended to my two other sisters, but when I asked her for the help I needed she refused me point blank. My child may have to go into care as we did not have anyone to look after her. I was beside myself with worry. I knew my husband needed to have this operation as soon as possible.

Then on Sunday morning, a church minister came and knocked at the door. I had forgotten I'd asked for communion, on that Sunday morning in hospital. I opened my door and let her in. She could see how upset I was. I explained to her what was happening.

She sat with me and asked me, "Avril, can you forgive your mother?"

I told her I could. She prayed for me, and I felt so much better.

Later on, the surgeon came to see me. He said, "Mrs. English, unfortunately because all the tests we have done on you have come back normal, you will have to ask us to take out your gall bladder. Is this something you want to do?"

I told the surgeon to take it out as anything was better than the pain I was in. I phoned my GP and told her what was happening. She told me to go ahead and have the operation and she would sort out my family situation. I was booked to go into theatre as soon as a slot became available.

The time came. They prepared me for theatre and began the surgery. However, during the operation they discovered I had chronic cholecystitis. This meant I had gall stones in my cystic duct and there was acute inflammation. They told me the stones were like diamond chippings which were rubbing together in the bile duct; this is what was causing me the severe pain. They also told me the stones were inside and outside the bladder.

After the operation, they took me down for an x-ray to make sure they had got all the stones out. I was in hospital a month in total. I was pleased when eventually I could go home. They told me I was not to do lifting of any kind including lifting the baby.

My husband delayed his appointment to go into hospital as he was taking care of our child. I decided to phone my Mum again in the hospital. I told her how sorry I was for speaking in the way I did. This was the first time we had ever fallen out. She told me she would come to look after the baby so that my husband could go into hospital and have his operation.

My husband had the operation on his neck. The surgeon told me they had got the lump in time, and he was going to be alright. The heavy burden of anxiety we had been carrying had been lifted from us both. Both of us were focusing on getting better. Mum went back to Blaydon, in Tyne-Wear and we managed things between us.

Chapter 12

Near Death

We were just getting back on track when we found ourselves in trouble once again. This time it was our daughter.

She was two and half years old at the time and we were celebrating Christmas with some friends. We placed nibbles onto the table, for our guests and for us to eat. One of the nibbles made our daughter unwell but we did not know which one it was.

We called the doctor who prescribed her antibiotics, but unfortunately her condition did not seem to improve. I had to call the doctor a number of times that day, as they wanted to know whether our daughter's condition was improving, unfortunately it was not.

Later on in the evening, the GP had to come out to us again. He put her on a nebulizer to see if it would help her breathing. He told me to ring him again if her condition became worse. In the early hours of the morning, I had to call the doctor out again.

This time the doctor was not going to take any more chances with her. He phoned for an ambulance. Her temperature was high, she was having difficulty breathing and she was hallucinating. The doctor told me there would be a team waiting for us when we reached the hospital. I had to get a message to my husband urgently to meet me at the hospital. I rang the police control room to get an urgent message to him and asked him to meet us at the hospital.

The ambulance arrived and now we were on the way to Royal Berkshire Hospital. We were meeting my husband there in the Emergency Department. The weather was terribly foggy and you could hardly see in front of you, I just hoped my husband was going to be okay driving in this weather. The ambulance crew were absolutely fantastic with our daughter, they kept her occupied until we arrived at hospital and in the Emergency Department. My husband arrived at the hospital the same time we did. At least now I would have the support I needed; I had never been so pleased to see him.

We were taken into a side room where the doctor began to examine our daughter. After the examination, the doctor told us if our GP had not got her into the hospital when he did, our daughter was within seconds of dying. She'd had a massive asthma attack, and he got her to the hospital just in time. The doctor put a canular in our daughter's hand so they could inject her with antibiotics and any other medication she may need. She was admitted onto the children's ward where she would be staying until they controlled her sickness. Both of us were devastated to learn what had happened to her. We were shocked at what the doctor had told us. We thanked our GP for saving her life.

I stayed in the hospital for several days with her until she was stabilized. The hospital gave me a room so I could stay in with my daughter. My husband was going to bring me the essentials I would need whilst I was in the hospital with her. I kept my husband updated with her progress.

Eventually, the hospital released her but they were making an appointment for us to go to a clinic so they could do allergy tests on her to see what our daughter was allergic to. She attended the clinic for them to do the allergy tests, and found she was allergic to many things. We were told that we would have to wash her favourite toys each day. I had to make sure I cleaned the house daily from top to bottom. We were told any visitors we had we had to tell them to have a bath and clean clothes on as this could affect her. Our daughter was allergic to nearly everything you could think of. This nightmare was getting bigger than we could have ever imagined. I know our friends understood what we had to ask them to do. I was embarrassed asking them to do this, but our daughter had to come first.

The doctors put her on a nebulizer, steroids and asthma medication. She had a peanut allergy which was one of the biggest allergies we had to avoid. She could not go near anyone eating peanuts. Animals were another thing she had to avoid, especially cat fur. At least we now had knowledge of what we should do in these circumstances for her. We had to keep an eye on her breathing too.

At least my little girl was not taken away from me, I had lost many children before we had her. I did not want to lose her as well.

Chapter 13

Born Again

John 3:3 NIV Jesus replied, "Very truly I tell you, no one can see the kingdom of God unless they are born again."

My grandmother was a Christian, and she was in the Scottish revival in the Hebrides. She had been married twice. Her first husband died in the war and left her raising five children. Then she met and married her second husband, and he died also in the war and left her with another five children. All in all, she was left to raise ten children from her marriages.

God helped her to cope and raise her children in a godly way. My granny was a very godly woman. She kept to the teachings of the Bible. She did not allow her children to do anything on a Sunday except to attend church three times.

She also prayed for all of her children, and when her children were married and had children of their own, she prayed for them too. God answered the prayers she petitioned on behalf of her children and grandchildren at His appointed time.

As children my siblings and I went to church because we wanted to. Mum did not force us to go, we went of our own accord. My younger brother and I were never christened because at the time we moved around a lot. Now both of us had decided that we wanted to be 'confirmed', but before we were able to do this we had to be christened. So, it was all arranged for us to be christened, followed by confirmation. Mum was going to be Godparent for us both. It all happened at a Church of England church in Newton Aycliffe.

I had been going to church up until the age of seventeen. I stopped going to church after I went to see my first fortune teller, this was when my life changed dramatically.

I can pinpoint exactly when my life began to go downhill. It was this moment, when I went to see my first fortune teller…

One day I was at work when my colleagues asked me if I wanted to go to a fortune teller with them. To be honest I did not want to go. When they suggested this to me, I felt really uncomfortable. One of the girls had been to see this fortune teller and she had convinced others that what this woman had told her was true. She continued to say that this woman had no idea what had happened to her in her life, yet she was coming out with things which she thought she could not possibly have known. The more she talked about what had happened to her, the more she convinced the others to go. They were curious and wanted to know what the fortune teller could tell them about their lives.

Anyway, to cut a long story short, because I did not want my colleagues to know the truth of how I was feeling when asked to go, I went along with them and told them I would go with them when they made the appointment.

At the time everything was arranged and the appointment made, we all went to see the fortune teller. We went into the room one-by-one. I was the last one to go into the room.

When the other girls came out of the room, they were full of it, telling the others what she had told them. When I went into the room, I thought I would not tell her anything about my life. She proceeded to tell me I was engaged to a soldier who was on duty abroad. She carried on to say that he was going out with another woman and was cheating on me. My ears pricked up when she began to talk about him. I felt sick at the things she was telling me. At the time I thought to myself how could she have known what was happening to me. She convinced me that what she was saying was absolutely true. She had drawn me in and the more she talked the more I listened.

The fortune teller had told me about what my fiancé at the time was doing. When he sent me a letter and a photograph with him and his friends on a night out together, I immediately saw that he was not wearing his engagement ring. I wrote to him and challenged him over this revelation I had seen. He did not deny it, so I ended my engagement to him. Everything the fortune teller had said to me, I convinced myself was true.

At the time I had no idea I had opened the door to demonic forces by going to her. I was ignorant and didn't know anything about occult forces. I just thought they were fictitious, but I learnt later on in life that I had allowed the devil's influences to come into my life without me knowing the truth about who he was and what he could do.

I found my curiosity deepen where these things were concerned. I began to see different spiritualists to see what they had to say to me. I got myself deeper and deeper into the occult. One day I had made an appointment to see a spiritualist.

The spiritualist told me I had a gift, and I had to develop the gift I had been given. I had no idea what this gift was. All I knew was that as a young child I had always felt there was something for me to do, but did not know what that was. So, when the spiritualist told me I had a gift, I was curious to know what this gift was. I wanted to try to develop the gifts I felt I was given. I had such a desire to help others.

Later on, a friend of mine gave me some tarot cards. For my 40th birthday my husband bought me a book called 'How to Read the Tarot Cards'. My friend and I were so pleased when I received this book, now we could learn how to read the cards together. I was saving this book to read when I went into the hospital for major surgery. I would read the book after my operation. However, God had other ideas (unbeknownst to me).

It was May 1988; my appointment had come through for me to go into hospital for major surgery. My husband and child took me into the hospital and onto the ward where a nurse was waiting for me to arrive. She took me to the bed where I would be staying for the next couple of weeks. I was admitted onto the ward, my suitcase unpacked, my husband picked it up to take it home, planning to bring it back to me when it was time for me to go home. He then left with my daughter and would return in the evening to see me before my operation the next day.

I settled onto the ward, the nurse had come and taken all my vital statistics, and finally I was ready for the operation the next day.

The following day came. I was on the list for theatre. I'd had my pre-med and was waiting for the porters to come and take me into theatre. I was wheeled into the theatre where the anaesthetist administered the general anaesthetic, and I knew nothing else about the operation. When I woke up, I was back on the ward recovering.

My husband had come into the hospital to visit me, but I was too groggy to realise he was there. He could see I was okay and needed rest. He kissed me goodbye and told me that he would come and visit me the next day.

The next day I was more alert. I was sore but I could cope with it. I looked diagonally across from my bed and saw a new face on the ward, a woman who hadn't been there before I went into theatre. I could see that she was struggling. I thought to myself I would go across to her bed and ask her if she needed anything. She asked me for a soda water, as she had heard that this helped with sickness. So, I gave her the drink she asked for and left her and went back to my bed. This was the beginning of our friendship.

One day my new friend and I were chatting, when I blurted out to her, "You are spiritual, aren't you?"

"Well," she said, "if you mean, 'am I a born-again Christian', and 'do I believe that Jesus Christ died on the cross for me, a sinner?' Then, yes, I am. Why Avril, do you not believe in the Lord Jesus Christ?"

My response to her was very indignant, and I replied to her, "Yes, I do!"

This was the moment my life changed.

My friend and I became closer. She told me that when she first came into hospital, she was on a different ward. At the time, she had prayed and told the Lord she knew He had sent her into the hospital to find someone, but felt the person opposite her there was not the one. She had her operation and when she woke up, she was on a different ward opposite me. She proceeded to tell me her operation had been cancelled three times.

Then I said to her, "That's funny, my operation also had been cancelled three times."

We both realized after talking with one another God wanted us in the hospital at the same time, and He wanted her to find me.

I had brought a number of magazines, plus the tarot book my husband had bought me for my birthday, into the hospital to read. I had hidden my book from my friend and had it in my locker. For some unknown reason I did not want her to see what I was reading. She also had brought a book into the hospital to read called: "God is Full of Surprises" by Gerald Hughes. Neither of us wanted the other to see the books we had - she also had placed her book into her locker as she did not want me to see the book she was reading.

One day God surprised us both. My new friend said to me, "Avril, you do know the book you are reading is evil?"

I thought about what she had said, and something within me knew what she was saying was right. A little later on I realized God was testing me to see what I would do.

When my husband came into the hospital with our daughter and friends to visit me, I had such an urgency to tell him to take the book, along with the tarot cards, home with him and that I wanted him to put the whole lot into the dustbin outside. I did not want them in the house when I got home. When I told my husband this, he thought I had gone mad and blamed the way I was behaving on my new friend. He felt that she had been influencing me in a wrong way. He had no idea what had happened to me in the hospital, but he could see something had changed.

My new friend and I began to pray for the patients that came onto our ward and the operations they were about to have. Praying seemed to help these people, although at the time I hadn't the foggiest idea what I was doing and who I was praying to. I would find out later on with God. I could see the prayers we had prayed God answered.

In the early hours of Sunday morning, I had woken up and found myself talking to God. (What God I had no idea). I told Him I was sorry for everything I had done in my life and would not interfere in anyone's life again.

I then began to cry uncontrollably, and I heard this still, small voice say to me, "Avril, everything that has been wrong in your life, I, the Lord your God, will put right."

My new friend came beside my bed after hearing me crying and asked me if I was alright. I told her what had just happened to me and all she said was, "Praise the Lord."

Chapter 14

God's Calling

1 Samuel 3:10 NIV The Lord came and stood there, calling as at other times, "Samuel! Samuel!" Then Samuel said "Speak, for Your servant is listening."

I had no idea what had happened to me, but things were about to get more interesting. I told my friend I was going to make a phone call to my husband and a friend.

I made the first call to my husband, then was about to make my second call when a voice in my head said, "Let the little old lady there use the phone."

I proceeded to say to the little old lady, "You can use the phone if you like, I need to sit down as I have just had an operation."

So, after being persistent, she used the phone. I sat down and waited for her to finish making her call. When you are in a public place it is inevitable that you hear bits of conversation from the person's phone call, although you don't wish to hear it. So, when the little old lady had finished her call, I found myself going up to her, putting my hand on her shoulder and saying to her, "You know, everything that has been awkward with today will be done tomorrow. You are to go now, close the door and have a good night's sleep."

She replied to me by saying, "You have been sent by God."

I replied to her and said, "Yes."

I could not believe what had just happened to me. I forgot about my other phone call and went back to my friend and told her everything that had happened. My new friend just smiled. I have to admit I was in a daze; I had no idea what was happening to me. It was so strange.

It was time for me to be discharged from the hospital. I said goodbye to my new friend, and we exchanged our addresses and phone numbers and promised we would keep in touch.

My husband took my name tag off the bottom of my bed and stuck the name tag onto my young daughter's jumper. We went and gave the medical staff a present and card my husband had bought for me to give to them for taking care of me in hospital.

My daughter and I held hands walking towards the lift to take us to the lower floor and to the way out of the hospital. We were in the lift when my daughter took the name tag off her jumper and placed the name tag onto my jumper, but the name tag was upside down, so I placed the name tag the right way up.

We got out of the lift, my husband was walking ahead of us when I heard this voice once again in my head say to me, "Avril, sit down on the bench."

The bench was outside of the chapel in Basingstoke Hospital. I shouted to my husband that I would be along in a minute. My daughter and I were chatting happily, people were passing by us when all of a sudden, the little old lady I had spoken to after her phone call stopped, smiled and looked at me.

"Ah - Mrs English!" She exclaimed, "That's your name!" She was looking at the name tag on my jumper. "I have been looking everywhere for you in the hospital. Everything you told me that day came to be. My husband had a massive heart attack, but he has come through!" She continued to say, "Mrs English, I will never forget you for the rest of my life."

We hugged one another and then I continued to walk out of the hospital with a new spring in my step. I felt happy and elated and I knew that God was calling me personally, as this was something that I had done on my own without my friend in the hospital being with me.

I just knew Jesus Christ was calling me to follow Him. Out of all the thousands of people in the hospital, God had led the little old lady and me to the seat at the chapel so that we could meet again. He wanted me to know that it was He who had arranged the meetings with the little old lady and my new friend so that I would know personally it was Him who was calling me.

I could not wait for the opportunity to phone my friend at home as soon as I was able to and tell what had happened when I left the hospital.

Chapter 15

Baptised

Romans 6:1-4 NIV What shall we say, then? Shall we go on sinning so that grace may increase? By no means! We are those who have died to sin; how can we live in it any longer? Or don't you know that all of us who were baptized into Christ Jesus were baptized into his death. We were therefore buried with him through baptism into death in order that, just as Christ was raised from the dead through the glory of the Father, we too may live a new life.

Life began to change radically for me. When I got back from hospital, I phoned my new friend and told her what had happened with the lady at the phone box. She seemed to be so pleased when I told her. Day by day I was beginning to feel stronger. The operation had really taken its toll on me, and I was unable to do anything very much within the home. I was doing what I was told to do by the consultants at the hospital. My body had to heal.

One morning I received a parcel from my friend from the hospital. Inside the parcel I had received four books and a letter with a verse of Scripture:

Psalm 139:13-16, "For You created my innermost being; You knit me together in my mother's womb. I praise You because I am fearfully and wonderfully made; Your works are wonderful; I know that full well. My frame was not hidden from You when I was made in the secret place, when I was woven together in the depths of the earth. Your eyes saw my unformed body; all the days ordained for me were written in Your book before one of them came to be."

I was blown away by these words, what a revelation God brought to me through His precious Word. I was so excited to know that I was with God in the beginning, that I had always been His child.

My friend gave me a Good News Bible and 'Everyday with Jesus'; a monthly devotional book to read daily alongside my Bible. It would teach me how to understand the Bible and hear God speak to me. Another book was 'My Father Is the Gardner,' by Colin Urquhart. This book showed me I needed and wanted the Holy Spirit of God. The final book was 'From

Witchcraft to Christ,' by Doreen Irvin. This book taught me about the demonic forces I had not recognized, and how I was in darkness and how powerful these evil forces could be.

In the letter, my friend said she hoped I enjoyed reading these books, and that the Holy Spirit of God had prompted her to send these books to me.

When I previously read the Bible in church in my early years of church life, the Bible did not make any sense to me. I thought it was a whole load of rubbish. I realise now how ignorant I was in my younger years; I did not understand the Bible because it had been hidden from me by God. It was when I acknowledged God as my Lord, Saviour and Redeemer and accepted that He died on the Cross for me a sinner, that I became a 'born-again' Christian.

When I was baptised in the name of God the Father, God the Son and God the Holy Spirit, I became alive in God. By acknowledging I was a sinner I came out from the darkness of the world and into the light with Jesus Christ. I could now understand through the Holy Spirit of God His Word. I was dead to sin, alive in Christ. Sin had no more hold on me when I admitted I was a sinner. Jesus Christ saved me and forgave me and set me free.

At the time of my acceptance of Christ, I still did not know the Holy Spirit of God personally. He was teaching me the truth about Jesus Christ, but I was not aware of His presence living in me at the time. I had not then acknowledged Him because I did not know about Him. The Bible spoke about the Holy Spirit of God, but I was still yet to understand He was a person, who I needed in my life too. I got to know my Heavenly Father, through Jesus Christ, now what I needed was to understand about the Holy Spirit of God as well.

Unbeknownst to me, the Holy Spirit was teaching me about the Godhead and the Trinity.

1 Peter 1:2 NIV says, 'Who have been chosen according to the foreknowledge of God the Father, through the sanctifying work of the Spirit, to be obedient to Jesus Christ and sprinkled with His blood. Grace and peace be yours in abundance.'

I began to read the Bible alongside the 'Everyday with Jesus' devotional. I found myself understanding what the Bible was saying to me, and bit by bit it became clear to me and started making sense. These books were a great blessing to me. No-one had done anything like this for me before and I could not wait to read them. I was like a sponge; I couldn't get enough of God. I felt so happy, happier than I had been in my whole life.

I began to read, 'My Father Is the Gardner, by Colin Urquhart. I found this book really inspiring. In the book, Colin was talking about the Holy Spirit of God. I wanted the Holy Spirit of God badly because Colin spoke how the Holy Spirit had changed His life, I wanted this Holy Spirit of God to change my life too.

I kept praying and praying, asking God to give me this Holy Spirit, even though I had no idea what it was.

Soon after, I had a phone call from my friend. She invited me to go to St. Peter's Church in Yateley, a Church of England church. She told me there was going to be a 'Ministry of Healing Service' on the Sunday, she thought I would like to go. I told her I would let her know. My husband had become difficult with my friend from the hospital. He had taken an instant dislike to her in the hospital. I was more enthusiastic than I had ever been before, and he could not understand the change that happened within me. My husband thought my friend in the hospital had been a bad influence upon me because I couldn't stop talking about Jesus and her.

Anyway, I asked my husband if I could go to the church and he said, "Yes I could go". I phoned my friend and told the good news that I could go. We made arrangements to meet her with her husband in Hook, Hampshire. I left my car in a safe place in Hook and went with them in their car to the church.

When we entered the church, I could hear a band playing. I had never been to a church where a band was playing before, there had only been an organist, when I went to church, this was entirely different to anything I had heard in a church before. I found it moving and exciting.

The moment the service began, it felt like God was speaking to me directly, and there was only Him and I in this place. He did this through the sermon the minister was giving. I began crying and did not have any control over my crying. I felt really embarrassed, as this went on through the whole service! After the service ended my friend spoke to me and said she felt the service was for me. I had to agree with her. I felt it too.

The minister addressed the congregation after the service and told the congregation they would continue to do a healing service. If anyone wanted to stay behind, they could, but for those who didn't want to stay behind for the healing service, he asked them to please leave the church quietly.

One by one, different people went forward for prayer. So, when my friend asked me if I wanted to go forward for prayer, I said yes. I was thinking I was going forward to help someone (because the spiritualist told me I had a gift and I had wanted to develop this gift I thought I had), but what I had not realised was that I was not going to help anyone, the person who was going to be helped would be me.

The minister and prayer team began praying for me. They asked me if I had been involved in the occult… My answer was I did not know. They continued in prayer, and number of the team who were praying began praying in a strange language. My friend explained to me afterwards the team were praying in the tongues of God, they were praying in God's language praying what He wanted them to pray for me.

1 Corinthians 14:4 NIV He who speaks in a tongue edifies himself, but he who prophesies edifies the church.

This Scripture was the confirmation I needed to know what had happened to me through my baptism was the tongues of God. The team continued in prayer, they asked me if I believed in the Lord Jesus Christ, that He died on the cross for me, a sinner.

I responded to the question, "Yes, I do".

Then the team proceeded to pray and began to baptize me in the name of the Father, and in the name of the Son, and in the name of the Holy Spirit. They prayed and asked God to fill me full of the supernatural power of the Holy Spirit of God. I was born again in the Spirit of Christ.

God had answered the prayer I had prayed for nights-on-end about receiving the Holy Spirit of God. I now too had the Spirit of God living inside of me as Colin Urquhart had. I left the church absolutely elated. I had never experienced anything like this before.

Chapter 16

God's Promise

Romans 10:17 NIV Consequently, faith comes from hearing the message and the message is heard through the word about Christ.

In my prayer time I heard the Lord say to me, "Avril, I am going to give you a gift of £5,000." I thanked God for the gift and continued on in prayer.

My friends from the flats became what I would call 'adoptive parents' to me. They were the first ones to hold my daughter after my husband and I when she was born. They now became her 'adoptive grandparents'. My husband and I treated them like parents and did what we were able to do for them as they did not have any children of their own.

They had been married later on in life and were unable to have children of their own. So, we made them part of our family and included them both in family events. They came to us for birthdays, Christmas, Easter, and any other celebrations we had. We wanted to include them in our family life. They were very special to me. They saw our daughter more than our own parents did.

It had been quite a number of months since God had spoken His word to my heart, when He reminded me about the gift He promised to give to me. I believed without a shadow of doubt He would do what He had said He would do.

In the November of 1990, my friend from the hairdressers came to see me. I was telling her about what God had told me He was going to do. I told her He was going to give me a cheque for £5,000. I showed her the entry I had made in my journal at the beginning of the year.

"Look," I said to her, "how daft am I? God said He was going to give me a gift of £5,000, and I was daft enough to believe Him."

She just looked at me and did not say very much.

As usual, God got the last laugh.

The very next day I had gone to visit my adoptive parents. We were chatting happily together when they said to me, "Avril, we want to give you an early Christmas present, for you and the family. We want you to take this with our love."

They wanted me to open the envelope and inside was a cheque for £5,000. I was in total shock. I did not know how to respond to this great gesture. They kept telling me they wanted us to have this gift, and they were really firm about this.

To be truthful, if God had not told me He was giving me a gift for £5,000 I would not have taken this gift no matter what they said. I received the gift with a grateful and thankful heart, knowing in my own heart, God had put this gesture upon their hearts to give this money to us. I praised and thanked God all the way home to my house and told my husband what had happened. When he looked into the envelope he was as shocked as I was. God's promise had come to pass. No-one had ever given us a gift like this before. We were both walking around in a daze.

We decided that we would put the money into buying a new car, as our car was on its way out. We found a car both of us liked. We told our adoptive parents what we were going to do, and they told us we must do what we thought was best for us.

One day I was going to my adoptive parents' for coffee. Out of the blue, my adoptive mum said, "Avril, I want Jesus in my life. Will you pray for me?"

I explained to her what it meant to receive Jesus Christ into her life, and she said she understood. So, I began to pray for her. I asked the Holy Spirit of God to put the words upon my tongue to pray for her. She confessed her sins and asked God to forgive her. I baptised her in the name of the Father, the Son and the Holy Spirit of God. Then I asked God to fill her full of His Holy Spirit from the top of her head to the tips of her toes, and come and reign in her heart. She had made her peace with God. Now, she too was born again in Christ. She looked absolutely radiant. Her husband had yet to make a commitment to the Lord, this came a bit later on in the story.

Chapter 17

Conversion

1 Peter 3:21 NIV And this water symbolises baptism that now saves you also — not the removal of dirt from the body but the pledge of a clear conscience toward God. It saves you by the resurrection of Jesus Christ.

It was January 1990; I received a phone call from my elder brother. He was asking me whether he could come and stay with our family at the weekend. He was working in Essex, not far away from where we lived. Of course I said yes, he could come.

At the time he rung me I was taking a bath. My husband had put a telephone in the bathroom so that if the phone rang, I could take the call, and I did not have to get out of the bath to answer it. My brother was telling me the story of working with two Christians in Essex. They had been talking to him most of the day about Jesus. One of the men owned the company he was working for. The other man who worked for him was also a Christian.

They were about to go home that evening when the owner of the company said to my brother, "You know, God will have the last laugh when He gets you."

My brother just laughed at them both and said to them, "He might."

Well God did get the last laugh with my brother. God really does have a great sense of humour. He used me in the next part of this story.

During the phone call, my brother said to me, "Mum told me that you are one of those Christians too?"

I answered him and said to him, "Yes, I am."

All he could say to this was, "Not another one!"

I told my brother how I became a Christian. I told my brother I met God in the hospital. I told him I spoke in a new language and continued to tell him I had written a book.

My brother could not believe what he was hearing. "You've what? Written a book and you speak a new language?"

I said yes to both questions. I continued and asked, "Do you believe in the Lord Jesus Christ?"

He replied, "Yes, I have always believed in Jesus since I was a child."

I continued and asked him, "Have you invited Jesus into your heart then?"

He responded to me by saying, "How do I do that?"

I said I would pray for him if he wanted me to. I told him I didn't know what I would pray, but I would trust God to put the right words on my mouth for him. He said he wanted me to pray so I did what he had asked.

So, I began to pray in the supernatural power of the Holy Spirit of God, He led me to ask my brother to pray the sinner's prayer. He did this and he was forgiven of all his sins.

Then I began to baptise him in the name of the Father, and in the name of His Son, and in the name of the Holy Spirit of God. I asked God to fill him so full of the Holy Spirit of God, cleansing him from all the sins, and wash and cleanse him through the blood of Christ, so he would be purified from all his sin.

I began to speak in the tongues of God, speaking directly to my brother's heart. I began translating the language I was speaking into English, so my brother could understand what God was saying to him. God was using me to be His instrument to reach my brother's heart.

At the time all this was happening, my brother was on the floor with his work phone. He truly was at the feet of Christ. My brother then said, "Avril, I cannot take any more of this, I will see you on Friday night."

We said our goodbyes to one another, and I put the phone down. I just began to chuckle and laugh at what God had done. I could see God's hand in all of this.

When my brother came to stay with me, he told me more of what had happened that night. He said he could not stop crying, he was unable to move for a number of hours and he felt so drunk he was unable to drive his car (this was so funny as my brother never drank in his life, he did not even like alcohol). He continued to tell me that he had missed his evening meal at the hotel, as he felt too drunk to drive. God really had taken the wind out of my brother's sails; He had hit him hard.

Matthew 28:19-20 NIV Therefore go and make disciples of all nations, baptising them in the name of the Father, and of the Son, and of the Holy Spirit, teaching them to obey everything I have commanded you.

Acts 2:38 NIV Peter replied, "Repent and be baptised, every one of you, in the name of Jesus Christ for the forgiveness of your sins. And you will receive the gift of the Holy Spirit."

When I went to bed that night, I was talking to God about what had happened that evening, and even when I was sleeping, I could see me laughing hysterically with the Lord. This will stay with me for the rest of my life. My brother had given his life over to the Lord. I was so happy God had used me in this way.

My prayer partner was coming to meet my brother the next day in the afternoon. When she came, I introduced her to my brother. Then, I felt God prompted me to say to them both we should both pray for my brother. We did this and my brother confessed in front of someone else publicly giving his life to God in front of her.

My brother's life changed radically from then on. He had a full-immersion water baptism, publicly giving his life to God, and someone within the church gave him words of wisdom confirming everything I had spoken to him in the tongues of God, when he gave his life to Christ. God had brought confirmation to my brother that what had happened to him was from God. I thanked and praised God for His faithfulness to me as I stepped out in faith in Jesus Christ my precious Lord.

Chapter 18

Mum's Death

John 5:24 NIV "Very truly I tell you, whoever hears My word and believes Him who sent Me has eternal life and will not be judged but has crossed over from death to life."

Our family was scattered all over the world and as a family we were always close. It was only when we got married things began to change and the resentments set in. My brothers and I resented the way my Mum treated us differently to our sisters' families. At the drop of a hat, any problems my sisters had, Mum went to them immediately. Yet, she did not do the same for my brothers and me. My sisters were the apple of my mother's eye.

My brother's children and my child she did not seem to notice much. This really hurt us. We always had to listen to Mum going on about our sisters' children, and the problems she had with them. I was the one she came to with all the problems she had.

Mum really did have a hold on me. She controlled and manipulated my life into the way she wanted it to be. My sisters also could persuade me to do what they wanted me to do. Now that I had a relationship with God, I could see what both my Mum and sisters had been doing. I should have stopped them controlling me a long time ago but at the time I did not know this was happening. I was a people-pleaser. I did not have the courage to stand against them. It was a lot easier just to do what they wanted.

Mum had phoned me up to ask me to take her place as she wanted me to go to Switzerland instead of her. Of course, this time I was able to say no to her as I had my own family to consider.

I received a phone call from my eldest sister telling me Mum had died that morning. She told me she was on the way to town to get last minute shopping to take to Switzerland. She had said goodbye to Dad and off she went to the bus stop. She got to the bus stop and then collapsed. An ambulance was called, and she was taken immediately to hospital. She had arrived at the hospital; the staff were unable to save her. She had died from a massive heart-attack. All the family were in total shock.

When I received the dreaded phone call, I was just about to pick my daughter up from school. I phoned my friend across the road and told her what had happened, and she took over from me. She was absolutely marvellous, how she handled the situation. She took control of my situation for me. She phoned another of our friends, told her what had happened and asked her if she was able to pick my daughter up from school. She phoned my husband at work and told him what had happened. He came home immediately.

My sister asked me if I could phone my sister in Switzerland and my brother in America. I did as she had asked and told them the news.

My brother in Darlington took the news a bit better than the rest of my family because he had Jesus in his heart. Jesus was helping him to cope with the situation. My brother and I prayed for the rest of the family. I was pleased he had a relationship with Jesus, same as me.

The dream I'd had many months previously had come to pass. This was the time when I was questioning whether the dream was from the devil or from the Lord. I now realise it was from God. God had been preparing me for this dreadful day. God had given me strength, grace, and peace, so when the time came for Mum's passing, I would be prepared to help the rest of the family.

Isaiah 41:10 NIV Fear not, for I am with you. Do not be dismayed. I am Your God. I will strengthen you; I will help you; I will uphold you with My victorious right hand.

The pain I experienced of losing Mum was one of the worst pains I could have ever imagined. Although my mum gave a lot of attention to my two sisters, in a funny kind of way Mum and I were closer together than they were. Mum always shared the problems she had with me and poured out her heart to me. I would listen to her and help her where I could.

God filled the emptiness in my heart, with the knowledge Mum was in the Kingdom of Heaven with Him. She had given her life to Jesus Christ the last time she was staying with me in Reading. Knowing Mum was born again in Jesus Christ helped me to cope with the situation. I was grieving for Mum, but in a strange way, I had been grieving for her when I had the dream many months before. In prayer I kept bringing the dream to Jesus about Mum. I did not realise it then that He had been preparing me before it happened. I would not hear my mum's voice ever again.

My adoptive parents had a Christmas card from my mum. On the front of the card was a dove with an olive branch in its mouth, with the verse:

John 14:27 NIV Peace I leave with you, My peace I give to you.

The words on the Christmas card, helped me in my grief, it was as if Mum was telling me through the words of Scripture she was at peace. It is as if she knew she was going to die. It would explain why she constantly asked me to go to Switzerland in her place, and also why she kept telling me she wanted me to have different things of hers. It was all falling into place now. I was so thankful to God for my adoptive parents, they gave me so much support and comfort just when I needed it.

The money they gave to us as an early Christmas present bought us the car we needed to go to the funeral. We took the family from Switzerland with us to attend Mum's funeral. We were picking my sister and her family up at Heathrow Airport, then going straight to the north of England.

My sister and her family were staying with Dad, my family were going to stay at my eldest sister's house. My brother and his family came to the funeral in Gateshead, Newcastle-upon-Tyne. My brother in America was unable to come to the funeral. We had to go ahead with the funeral without him.

Mum was going to be cremated; this is what she wanted. The day came when we were all going to the crematorium. She was not going to have a church service beforehand.

My elder sister and her husband had done all the preparations for the funeral. They had arranged for a minister to be used at the crematorium to take the service. Mum's family had been informed of her death and some of Mum's relatives were going to attend the funeral. My uncles and cousins came from Inverness in Scotland.

The day was here. Everything had been prepared. I was totally numb inside.

The funeral was a real disappointment to me. It was not the kind of service I wanted for Mum. It was dead. My elder sister and brother-in-law were not born in the Spirit of God, so the service was not centred on God. It was like a meat market. Mum had come into the building, the service was done, and then we were shown out of the Crematorium for the next funeral to take place.

My sister always took control of everything. She and her husband did not listen to anything I had said, or had asked them to do, which I had felt the Lord wanted me to tell them to do. They just went ahead and did the funeral the way they wanted it done. I tried to remember they did not have a relationship with Jesus Christ, I asked Jesus to help me to forgive them. I could see that my sister and her husband had arranged the funeral in a worldly way.

After the service we had gone to Dad's house where food had been prepared by the caterers. Everyone was chatting about Mum, but I did not want to talk with anyone, so I hid away from the people and found a place in Dad's house where I did not have to have conversations with them.

Our doctor, a family friend, also attended the funeral as he had always been close to Mum. I felt alone and this was one of the saddest times of my life. I did not want to talk to anyone after the funeral.

The funeral was over. My sister from Switzerland and her family were going to stay with us for Christmas. We stayed on another couple of days, then it was time for us to go home to Reading. We decided we would try and make Christmas nice for our two children. We had a nice time together as best we could under the circumstances, and then it was time for my sister's family to go home to Switzerland.

God helped me in the days ahead in my grieving period. I know one thing for certain, if I did not have God in my life, I would never have coped with my Mum dying. Each day my heart began to become lighter. Jesus was helping me to cope with my grief and sorrow. It was a process I had to go through. It had to take its course. I prayed for the whole family daily, for God's grace, mercy, strength and love to help them through. They did not have a personal relationship with Christ, so they needed prayer, I asked Jesus to rescue and save them from the world and to bring each and every one of them through at His appointed time. I did not want any one of them to be missing on the day of salvation.

My Dad would not allow me to speak to him about Mum. I could not understand why he did this with me. He allowed the rest of the family to talk about Mum to him, but he did not allow me to. I found this devastating. It was another rejection I had to take on board. I found he had treated me differently from the way he treated the rest of my siblings, and I just could not understand why he treated me like this.

My elder brother was praying for the family as well. We both had a strong faith in God, but the rest of the family did not have a faith or relationship with the Lord Jesus Christ, unfortunately they lived their lives in the world. We prayed God's salvation would come to each one of our family and that not one of them would be missing on the day of salvation, that God would redeem and save them too as He had saved and rescued my brother and me.

Chapter 19

I Will Restore

Jeremiah 30:17 NIV 'I will restore you to health and heal your wounds, declares the Lord.'

I was recovering bit by bit after the loss of my Mum. God was strengthening me to overcome.

It was now March 1991; I had a lump come up in my neck. The doctor sent me to hospital to see a consultant and the consultant decided they would take the lump out of my neck.

An operation was planned and took place in June. The surgeon took the lump out and it was sent away to be analysed. The results came back negative, the lump was not sinister.

Not long after my operation, my daughter came out in a rash over the lower part of her body. My husband and I thought it was chickenpox. I took her to the doctors and got some heart-wrenching news. The doctor said it wasn't chickenpox, he thought it was purpura, which occurs when small blood vessels leak blood under the skin. He showed me a picture from his medical book and did the test on my daughter. It showed me she had identical symptoms to what the doctor was showing me in the book. I asked the doctor if there was a cure for this. His response to me was that there is no cure.

He took some blood tests from her and told me to come back for the results the following week, I was told not to allow her to exert herself in any physical activity whatsoever. I had to keep her quiet and not allow her to do any activities whatsoever. I told my husband what the doctor had said, and he was shocked at the diagnosis we had been given. I prayed over my daughter and felt I should ask my husband for permission to take her to the church at Three Mile Cross, to have her prayed for. I had faith in God and if it was God's desire to heal and help my daughter then I wanted her to be prayed for. My trust and faith were in God.

My husband did not object to me taking her to church. So, my prayer partner and I made an appointment with the minister as soon as possible.

I told the minister what was going on with my daughter and he agreed we could bring her to the church where he would pray over her with us. We were taken to a room where we all prayed for her. Those prayers were answered, all glory to God.

Within one week of petitioning our requests to God, Jesus answered our prayers. Every single bit of rash disappeared completely from her body. I had already made the appointment at the doctors to receive the results of her blood tests.

When I took her into the doctor's room, he couldn't believe his eyes... Every bit of the rash he had seen the week before on her body had gone completely. I told the doctor what had happened and that I had taken her to the church to have her prayed over. The doctor's response was to tell me it would come back again.

I told the doctor, "Oh no. It won't come back. If God wants to heal someone, He doesn't do half a job."

I knew by faith God had healed her completely. He had granted us another miracle over her life. I gave Him all the glory, honour and praise. I was so grateful and thankful to Him for what He had done for our child. I had trusted God this purpura would not come back because Jesus had healed her completely.

Chapter 20

Dad's Death

John 14:1-2 NIV "Do not let your hearts be troubled. You believe in God, believe also in Me. My Father's house has many rooms; if that were not so, would I have told you that I am going there to prepare a place for you?"

My eldest sister and her family had gone to their holiday home in Spain. They had asked Dad if he wanted to go with them, but he declined the invitation. He was not keen on going abroad at any time as he had enough of travelling abroad when he was in the army. So, I told my sister not to worry, to go on her holiday and I would keep an eye on Dad.

I phoned Dad after my sister had left. He said he was fine, and I was not to worry. A couple of days later I phoned him again but was unable to get a response from him. I tried to reach him a number of times, but he wasn't picking up. I was starting to get a bit anxious. I decided to ring my brother in Darlington, as he did not live too far from Dad. It would take him about three quarters of an hour to get to Dad's to make sure he was all right.

My elder brother was very worried about Dad, so he decided he would phone the police and ask them if they could check up on Dad to make sure he was alright. The police did go to Dad's house, and when they arrived, they found Dad outside in the garden checking his vegetables! He took great pride in his garden. Dad was okay, so at least I could rest knowing he was fine.

My husband had booked a four-day holiday in Torquay in Devon. We thought it would be nice to spend some quality time together. With my husband's job, he did not get much time off. So, this was one way we could have our family time together. We rang and told Dad we were going to Devon for a few days, but we would ring him each night whilst we were away to make sure he was okay. He replied that this would be fine.

I had a deep desire to write to Dad and ask him to forgive me for the way I had treated him. I felt he treated me differently to the rest of my siblings and I had built up resentment and bitterness in my heart towards him over the years.

Having a relationship with the Lord Jesus Christ showed me how wrong I had been towards my dad, and I wanted to put things right between us, so I hoped the letter I had written to him would do just that.

On the 4th of August 1991, Mum and Dad would have been married over fifty years. I had bought him a card for his wedding anniversary and put the letter inside the card. I wanted him to get the letter and card whilst we were away.

My elder brother had made arrangements to be with Dad whilst we were away. He was going to see him on the Monday night after finishing work. Dad and my brother had always got on well together. When my brother was younger, he worked with Dad as an electrician on the site where my dad worked. They lodged together in the same lodgings. So, their relationship worked well, and they always enjoyed each other's company.

We arrived at our hotel in Devon, and I phoned Dad to tell him we had all arrived safely, I did not want to take up too much of his time as he was expecting my brother that night.

When I rang Dad on the Tuesday night, Dad seemed happy, and he told me everything that happened when my brother had seen him. My brother was an evangelist and always wanted to tell the Good News about Jesus Christ to others. My brother began to tell Dad how Mum had given her life to Jesus when she visited me in Reading. Dad said to him Mum hadn't mentioned this to him. My brother went to his car to get my baptism tape so Dad could listen to it. In the meantime, Dad was looking for his cassette player so they could play the tape on but unfortunately he couldn't find it. So, my brother suggested they could go and listen to the tape in his car and two of them went and did this.

Dad was asking my brother all kinds of questions about the water baptism tape. To the best of his ability my brother answered his questions. I chuckled to myself after the conversation I'd had with Dad about my brother. God was truly a gracious God, my brother doing this meant so much to me. At least Dad would have heard the gospel. We said goodnight to one another, and I told him I would ring him the next evening.

I phoned Dad the next evening, but I did not get any response from him. I tried to ring him numerous times but still no answer. We were going home the next day so my husband told me to wait until we got home then I could try and ring him again. I did not get the opportunity to ring Dad. My older brother rang me first and told me Dad had died. He explained what had happened to him.

Once again, I was in shock. He continued to tell me that the neighbour across the road from Dad saw his light on all night into the morning, when they got up. They thought this was strange, so they phoned the police, who came straight out to Dad's house where the neighbour met them to give them the key to get into Dad's house.

When the police went into Dad's house they called out to Dad, but got no answer from him. They continued to look around the house and they could see a window had been broken in the sitting room. They went into the hallway, and Dad was at the bottom of the stairs. They found him dead. The police think Dad must have been going upstairs to bed when he had fallen backwards down the stairs.

When they did an autopsy, they found Dad had a massive stroke and he died instantly. He had been dead for quite a while before he was found. This had been the reason why I could not get him on the phone.

This was a great shock to me. It was bad enough Dad dying but having the knowledge that someone was trying to break into his house as well did not help matters. It had not been that long since we had lost Mum, now we had lost Dad too.

The rest of the family needed to be informed. The hardest thing we had to do was get in touch with my sister in Spain. We did not have an address or phone number for her. The rest of the family had been informed. Now we had to wait until my sister was informed in Spain.

In the meantime, my elder brother took control of arranging the funeral. My brother had spoken to someone he knew in his church who gave him the phone number of a pastor who lived near to Dad. The church was a free church in Winlaton, Newcastle-Upon-Tyne. The free church was near to where Dad lived. An appointment was made for my brother to meet with the pastor at the church. My brother discussed the kind of service he wanted for Dad. He also suggested to the pastor he wanted me to take part in the funeral service. I nearly fainted and was shocked my brother had said this to him. I told my brother I could not do this. God had other ideas for me. He sent a methodist minister to my home. I told the minister what was going on, and he turned round and encouraged me and said, "Avril, you can do this." He gave me an order-of-service booklet for me to look at, and also prayed God's will upon the situation.

In the meantime, my brother phoned me and told me the pastor from the church wanted me to phone him. I had prayed constantly about the situation and what I was being asked to do. I wanted the sovereign will of God on this, and did not want to do anything in my own strength.

God had equipped and empowered me with everything I needed to tell the pastor what I felt God wanted me to do within the service. I was so sure-footed about this service; God had given me everything I needed to do what He was calling me to do.

When the pastor rang me later, I told him what I felt the Lord wanted me to do. I was so sure-footed about this that both he and his wife got on their knees before God and went into prayer over the situation. The pastor told me this after the funeral had taken place.

I was absolutely depending and leaning on God. I had never done anything like this before. I did not like speaking in public places, never mind being part of a funeral service. I had always felt inadequate, but I trusted God in all of this, and knew if I was to do this then He would anoint me to do this great task.

The funeral service was going to take place at Winlaton Free Church, on the 15th of August 1991, and afterwards we were going to the crematorium at Gateshead where the pastor would hold a short service. This was the same place Mum had her service when she died.

I met the pastor at the church before the service began. He told me what he wanted me to do. Everyone was settled within the church and the pull bearers brought Dad into church. The family was settled in, and the pastor began the service.

That day is a day I will never forget for the rest of my life. The pastor introduced me during the service. He said, "Mrs. Avril English is to be highly commended today, this is the first time any woman has been in the pulpit apart from pastor and myself."

I was absolutely shocked. I did not expect the pastor to say this. I had no idea I was the first woman they had in the pulpit. I went forward into the pulpit and did what God had called me to do. After I had finished doing what I was called to do, I sat down, and the pastor continued on with the service.

He began to address each and every member of my family individually. The Holy Spirit of God used the pastor to speak directly to my brothers and sisters individually. I was amazed at what came out of the pastor's mouth; it was God's Holy Spirit using him to talk to my brothers and sisters about their lives. I knew what he was saying about them was absolutely true and my siblings knew it too. God was the One who spoke to my family about their lives, and He used the pastor as a vessel to do it.

When the service had finished, my elder sister came up to me and said, "Avril, I couldn't have done what you have just done." I never thought I would hear words like this from her. I had always felt inadequate around her because of her education, as she was a university lecturer, and I had no qualifications whatsoever. The important thing to me was I had obeyed God and done what He had called me to do. Nothing else mattered.

We left the church and now we were on the way to the crematorium, where the pastor was taking the service there. I felt God was putting things right because of the funeral service we had for Mum at the same crematorium. He was putting her funeral right. It was a wonderful service we had for Dad. The pastor included Mum within Dad's service.

My elder sister was going to collect Dad's ashes, and we were going to buy a plaque for both Dad and Mum, to have in the Crematorium for always.

I met the pastor later on after the service. He told me what had happened after I telephoned him and told me that he and his wife, got down on their knees before God and asked God if this is what He wanted me to do at the funeral. He told me I was so sure-footed, full of confident faith that after praying about the whole situation to God, he knew God wanted me to do this.

In the evening at my elder sister's house all of my family celebrated Mum and Dad's life on the earth. In a strange kind of a way we were all joyful and we knew Mum and Dad would have liked us to celebrate and be happy for them. At least they both were in the Kingdom of Heaven with God, as they had both committed their lives to God in Jesus' name before they died.

Chapter 21

A Dream

Genesis 15:1 NIV After these things the word of the Lord came to Abram in a vision saying, "Do not fear, Abram, I am a shield to you. Your reward shall be very great."

I had been praying to the Lord, asking Him to give me confirmation that Dad had reached the Kingdom of Heaven. I committed it to God and left it with Him.

A little later, my sister and I were clearing Dad's house out. There was a three-piece suite, which we offered to a lady who was a friend of our parents.

While we were at their home, their little daughter began to talk. She told us she'd had a dream, and in the dream she saw my mum waiting at the gates of heaven, calling to my dad to come home. I was absolutely amazed when this young girl came out with these words.

Unbeknownst to her, she had brought me the answer to my prayer. I was elated when she told me this - at least my parents were together again. God again in His faithfulness had answered my prayer.

My brothers took what they wanted from our parents' estate. My sister in Switzerland had Mum's cookbooks; these were the only things she was able to take with her to Switzerland. My sister-in-law's behaviour was abominable. She wanted everything she could lay her hands on. I did not like her behaviour, and I told her so.

We had a certain amount of time to clear the house out. We gave most of my parents' things to charity, hoping they would go to good use. It was hard, getting rid of all of Dad and Mum's memories; things they had worked hard for all their lives, and now those things meant nothing because Dad and Mum were not here any longer.

We were devastated that Mum and Dad had gone from the earth, but at least they had gone home to be with Jesus. This brought comfort to my heart. He was the only One who could help me get through this terrible time.

I leaned and depended upon God for everything. It was hard going. It was bad enough losing Mum in the December time, now I was grieving the loss of Dad too.

My eldest sister was the executor of our parents' will. When the will was completed, we received a letter each from her. Inside the letter was a cheque for each of us - a share in my parent's estate. I was thankful for the gift I received.

Chapter 22

Life Continues

Philippians 1:21 NIV For to me, to live is Christ and to die is gain.

I continued on with my journey with God. I was still grieving over the loss of my parents, but God was helping me in my grief.

Day by day, I prayed and read the scriptures and felt close to God. I needed God daily in my life. Without Christ in my life, my life meant nothing. To live in Christ meant I had to die to the world. Jesus Christ was my everything.

I continued being a housewife to my husband, and mother to my child. I made sure they both had everything they needed. God was delivering me from my past bit by bit, and He was removing the darkness I had touched before I knew His name. I wanted more of God, and less of me. God was the most important person in my life. I wanted to do things the way He was showing me to do things, a bit at a time, at a pace I could handle.

God's Holy Spirit was changing my thought pattens into the thoughts of Christ. He was showing me where I needed to change.

I dedicated my life to God by submitting, surrendering, and relinquishing my life to Him daily. I wanted His Holy Spirit to direct my footsteps into His sovereign will. He had a plan for my life, and I did not want to hinder God's plans He had made for me.

He was in control of everything I did. I did not want to walk in the ways I had walked before I knew His name. I continued to go to church, led by the Holy Spirit of God.

God was teaching me He did not want me to leave my husband out of what I was doing, and to consider him in everything I was doing. My husband was as important to God as I was.

One day whilst I was praying, the Lord gave me a great big challenge. He said to me, "Avril, if you cannot obey your husband, then you cannot obey Me." I was shocked when I heard God speaking these words to me. I have to admit, before I knew Jesus personally, I was a rebellious and stubborn wife. I needed to change my attitudes towards my husband.

So, when God spoke these words to my heart, I responded to Jesus and said, "Lord, I will win my husband to Christ in my obedience to him." I prayed and asked Jesus to change my attitudes, and enable me to be the kind of wife and mother He wanted me to be. I'd asked Jesus to put right the mistakes I had made with my husband, child, and others. I asked Him to heal my hurt and pain. Jesus has healing power to set me free for everything I had done which had been wrong. I know things would not be put right instantly, but I did know with Jesus' help, bit by bit, I would be healed from everything.

Genesis 50:20 NIV You intended to harm me, but God intended it for good to accomplish what is now being done, the saving of many lives.

Chapter 23

Confidence in Christ

Philippians 1:6 NIV Being confident of this, that He who began a good work in you will carry it on to completion until the day of Christ Jesus.

My confidence in Jesus Christ was growing daily. I could never thank God enough for everything He was teaching me. I had never felt love such as that which God was giving to me. His love and forgiveness, His grace and mercy, was a lot to take on board. Of all the things I have experienced in my life, Christ's forgiveness went beyond anything I could have ever known or imagined.

I remember God woke me up one morning. My whole bedroom was filled with light. This had only happened once before, when Mum had died, and Jesus came to me to bring me comfort through my loss.

Anyway, Jesus asked me, "Avril, do you love Me?" I was shocked when He asked me this question. I thought to myself how on earth am I going to respond to this question? I did not want to lie.

So, I responded to Him truthfully. "How can I love You Lord, when I don't know what love is?" Jesus then said to me that He was love. He was asking me question after question, and I answered Him to the best of my knowledge and ability. For every question He asked me, He comforted me with His answers and was changing and healing my heart.

Then I had a vision from God. Jesus was holding up a golden jug over me. He was pouring gold liquid into me, and this liquid was never ending. The gold liquid felt warm and loving. I was overwhelmed by His actions. Instead of me always giving to others, now God was giving to me His love. I felt so much love in my heart, it was overflowing like a stream of water washing over me. This was warm and comforting. Every time I felt unloved and rejected, the Holy Spirit of God, reminded me the love Jesus had for me and His love is never ending. He was not going to allow the enemy to take this blessing from me.

Isaiah 43:19 NIV See, I am doing a new thing! Now it springs up, do you not perceive it? I am making a way in the wilderness and streams in the wasteland.

2 Corinthians 5:17 NIV Therefore, if anyone is in Christ, the new creation has come. The old has gone, the new is here.

Chapter 24

Negativity

Philippians 4:8-9 NIV Finally, brothers and sisters, whatever is true, whatever is noble, whatever is right, whatever is pure, whatever is lovely, whatever is admirable - if anything is excellent or praiseworthy - think about such things. Whatever you have learned or received or heard from Me or seen in Me - put into practice. And the God of peace will be with you.

God was showing me I had allowed myself to become negative. Actually, I had been negative until the day I became a Christian. The Holy Spirit of God began to bring the truth into my heart. He opened my eyes to see what He wanted me to see, and He opened my ears to hear what He wanted me to hear. He showed me I must not allow people to give me negative thoughts. He wanted me to study the Bible and look for the truth in the Bible. He wanted to influence my life, and He did not want man/woman to influence me. I had to walk in obedience and trust Him to do what was right and necessary for me to grow in Jesus Christ.

Jesus was shining His light into the dark places of my soul. He was freeing me from all the influences I had allowed into my life. He was changing me from the inside out. I did not like what I had been and really did want to change, so I asked Jesus to change me and become all that He had created me to be. Jesus was the only One who had the power to remove those influences from my life and set me free completely. I was going to rely upon, lean upon, and depend upon Him for everything I needed. I wanted to obey the words written in the Bible. I kept relying upon the Holy Spirit of God to change me to be more Christ-like. All I had to do was allow Jesus to have the access to my heart, spirit, and soul He would do the rest.

The enemy had lied to me and controlled my life for forty years, now I wanted Jesus to control the rest of my life until the day I died. No more was I going to allow the enemy to control me. I was not going to listen to his lies any longer.

I have learnt if you listen to the wrong kind of counselling or teachings, they can and will affect your life. I have learnt to sit and be quiet before God, listening to His gentle voice, He has taught me to look into the Word of God

(Bible), and pray to Him to find the truth. He leads me through the Holy Spirit of God and He brings the truth into my heart and mind. I have the Helper, Comforter, Teacher, the One sent to guide and lead us into all truths. He is the Only One who helps me.

God's peace destroys all doubts, fears and negativity. If you lose that precious gift of peace, you know something is not quite right, and it's the Holy Spirit of God trying to tell you something. You must ask Him if you have stepped out of God's will.

I had asked Jesus to bring positive things into my life and enable me to grow in faith. Jesus has been breaking down and uprooting the strongholds through which I had allowed the power of the enemy to influence my life.

Prayer is the most powerful thing I have learnt. I prayed and asked Jesus to bind and block this spirit of negativity on earth as it is in heaven, and for Jesus to set me free from this darkness once and for all (see Matthew 18:18 NIV). I believed Jesus had done what I had asked of Him, and I was now free from all negativity.

The old things had passed away. Now, I was excited about those new things Jesus was doing for me.

Chapter 25

Back to Work

Acts 6:7 NIV So the word of God spread. The number of disciples in Jerusalem increased rapidly, and a large number of priests became obedient to the faith.

I felt the Lord was going to send me back to work. I applied for a part-time job when my daughter began to attend senior school. I felt it was time to do something that would challenge me. I applied for a job at Asda supermarket as a check-out operator. I went for an interview, but the job which was offered to me was not on the checkouts, but a position in Human Resources. I had never done this kind of work before, but I knew if God wanted me to do this kind of job, then He would equip, enable and empower me to do the job.

I had no idea how this was going to work out. My hours of work were from Monday to Friday, 9am until 2pm. The days and hours suited me fine. I would be able to keep on top of things, be at home for my husband and child as I did not want work to interfere with my family life.

My husband bought me a Ford Escort car which I travelled to work in. It was an older car, but it was ideal for doing short trips to and from work. I was happy with it.

I began to learn the new job. I prayed each morning before I went to work. I did not want my day to begin without including God in the centre of my day. I made sure I got up early so I could pray and read God's Word beforehand. It had always been important to me to include the Holy Spirit of God and allow Him to be in control of my life. I had to allow Him access to every part of my life. He helped me to handle whatever situations would arise within the day. I prayed about every single task I had to learn.

Prayer and studying the Word of God came first; I needed God's wisdom, understanding, insight, discernment and revelation to help me accomplish what He wanted me to accomplish with the people I was working with.

The people I worked with in personnel, were difficult to work with. They had been working in the department for many years, and they did not like new blood coming into their workplace. They were being difficult in showing me the job. I knew the enemy did not want me to work there, God helped me to handle the people I worked with. Before I knew Jesus Christ, this situation would have really troubled me and made me feel inadequate, especially as this job was different to any other job I had done. But with Christ living within me I knew He would equip and empower me, and I would do the job. I leaned upon, relied upon, and depended upon Him for everything I needed.

I forgave the women I worked with because they did not have a relationship with Jesus Christ. I was not going to hold any grudges or resentment against them.

God gave me an opportunity and made the way clear for me to speak to the girls I worked with. I gave a testimony about what Jesus did for me and what He could do for them too. I did not force my love and faith upon them, I hoped that they could see something in me that was different to them and want what I had in Jesus Christ. I spoke out with confidence and faith when the opportunities arose. I did not allow their jealousy to get in the way of me doing God's will. I was put in this place by God, and I persevered in the job because this is what God wanted me to do. No man would put asunder what God had ordained me to do for the glory and praise of Christ Jesus.

The manager told us all that they were going to use a new system, putting the payroll onto computers. I was really pleased about this, as I had experience with computers previously. I was computer literate. I found using computers a simple way of doing the payroll and grasped the work quickly. The women I worked with had no experience working on computers, so I taught them the system. I had God on my side, and He helped me and equipped me to do this work in the store.

The store manager decided I was going to work with him as well as in personnel. He thought he could use the skills I had to do the work he needed to be done. I enjoyed the work I was doing for him, and he was pleased with the work I did for him.

Daily, I prayed about the store, the colleagues and the managers. God was giving me the discernment needed to pray about the store-managers and colleagues.

The store managers did not treat the colleagues respectfully. They were not civil to them when they asked them to do things needed in the store. My colleagues were unhappy with the way they were treated. So, I spoke to God about how the managers were treating the colleagues, and things began to change. One by one each of the managers were moved onto different stores. This was a good result, my prayers for the colleagues had been answered in a dramatic way. Each person on earth has a job to do. It does not matter what that job may be, it is important to God. Just because managers have been given the authority over departments and the workers in those departments, does not mean they should be disrespectful towards the work that they do. They should encourage the staff that work under them. Some people think that because they are in a higher position in the store, they can treat colleagues badly and unfairly, and not provide opportunities for them to excel in the workplace.

God kept bringing individual people to me. These people poured their hearts out to me, and afterwards I would pray about their situations, and asked God to help them and change the situations they were in. I could see God's faithfulness in how He answered the prayers I petitioned for the people I prayed for.

The truth would set these people free if they wanted it. I know what Jesus did for me, He could do for them. I was happy and contented, but I did need Jesus each day to help me in my workplace, as the enemy was constantly on my back because of my love for Jesus.

I felt God was going to lead me in a different direction. He wanted me to give up my job at the Asda superstore, and give my attention to my adoptive parents. I also wanted to spend as much time as I could with my daughter as it would not be long before her education at senior school would end, and she would go on the next stage of her life. So, because family was important to me, I did what was asked of me, and I was going to make the most of the time I had with them.

Avril English

Chapter 26
My Adoptive Parents

John 3:3 NIV Jesus replied, "Very truly I tell you, no one can see the kingdom of God unless they are born again."

I had finished working at Asda and I focused my attention on the family. I was taking my adoptive Mum to get her weekly shop. We had just finished shopping at the local supermarket when suddenly she had a terrible pain in her chest and back. Thank God the doctors' surgery was just down the road! I got her into the car and took her straight to the surgery. I told the receptionist what had happened, her doctor was in the surgery and immediately the receptionist brought a wheelchair to take her in to see her doctor where the doctor examined her. Her GP told me she needed to go into hospital straight away. The doctor rung her husband and explained to him what had happened to her. The doctor told him that I was on my way to pick him up, and to put a few things in a bag for her so she would have what she needed in the hospital. When I picked him up, I told him what had happened. We put the shopping away, especially the things for the fridge and freezer, then went straight back to the surgery. We arrived at the same time as the ambulance. My adoptive dad went into the ambulance with his wife. I followed the ambulance in the car and would meet them at the hospital.

I had arranged with my husband to pick our daughter up from school, and told him what had happened. I would be home as soon as things were sorted out at the hospital. All the way to the hospital I was praying in the Spirit of God, asking God to take care of them both. I knew my adoptive dad would be upset at what had happened, they were so close to each other and had been married over forty years. The doctor told us he thought she'd had a heart attack.

I was so grateful and thankful to God for His faithfulness to me. He really did make sure my needs were met, if I had not had Him in my life goodness knows how I would have coped with the situation I was in. I was so grateful and thankful to God for His help and support. The hospital examined her, and they did various tests upon her and found she did have a heart attack. We stayed with her until we knew she was settled, and when the time was right, we went home. We told her we would be in the next day, and bring in the things she would need in the hospital. She needed to rest.

When we got home, we packed a number of things to take to the hospital the next day. I asked my adoptive dad if he was going to be okay, and he said, "Yes". I arranged a time with him when I would pick him up. We went to the hospital daily until she was allowed to go home.

On Sunday morning I received a phone call from her husband. He said to me, "I've done it."

I responded to him with, "You've done what?"

He said, "I've given my life to Jesus Christ this morning." He continued to say, "I got down on my knees and asked God to forgive me my sins and asked Him to come into my heart." Wow, I was so happy for him. I believe God used what happened to his wife to get him to cry out to God.

When we went into hospital to visit her, he told her what he had done. We were so happy that now we all were born again in Christ. Once again in God's faithfulness He had answered our prayer requests. His wife's health improved, and the doctors told her she could go home. We were all so thankful that God had healed her.

Life continued on. My adoptive mum was beginning to show signs that she had dementia. This was hard for her husband to cope with. He became my adoptive mum's full-time carer. I helped him to cope as best I could. I would sit with her whilst he went out to have a break. When it became too difficult for him the doctor put her into respite care at Dellwood Hospital, Liebenrood Road, Tilehurst, for a week at a time. He would go to Devon to be with his nieces, where they would look after him while I looked after her visiting her daily, and doing her washing and ironing. I updated him with her progress and told him he need not be worried as his wife was getting the best possible care.

He came back from Devon having been rested. They both had the rest they needed until she had to go into care again.

Chapter 27

God's Kingdom

John 14:2 NIV My Father's house has many rooms; if that were not so, would I have told you that I am going there to prepare a place for you.

Life continued on and my adoptive mum's dementia was deteriorating. Dellwood Hospital in Tilehurst was unable to take her in for respite care any longer. The doctors were referring her to a psychiatric hospital on the outskirts of Reading. She was going to have her respite at this hospital.

An appointment with the consultant had been made, and my adoptive dad told the consultant that he wanted me to attend the appointment as he would be away in respite in Devon. To be truthful he could not cope with what was wrong with his wife, so he wanted me to attend the appointment instead of him with the consultant.

The day came for me to attend the appointment with the consultant. They told me they thought it was best if she went into full-time care. So, this is what they wanted to do. I phoned up her husband and told him the outcome of the appointment.

Things were about to change for both of them. An appointment had been arranged with a social worker to come and speak to him about a care home. He wanted me to attend the appointment with him. When the social worker suggested places where his wife could go, they were too far away for him to visit her.

I kept praying about the best home for her to go to. God again was helping me. My prayer partner suggested the Hollies Nursing Home in Burghfield Common. I talked this through with him and told him what was suggested to me. So, after our conversation about the Hollies Nursing Home, he wanted my prayer partner and I to go and make an appointment with the matron at the home and talk it through with her. At the time this was going on, my adoptive dad was in Devon on respite.

We both attended the appointment together and we discussed the situation with the matron. Although they did not usually take in dementia patients, the matron decided she would take his wife in.

This was a great answer to prayer. At least her husband would be just around the corner from her, and he would not have to go far to see her. I could take him, and we could go together. I had to discuss this outcome with him when he came home from Devon. They wanted him to see the room where she would be and if he thought it was right for his wife.

When he came home from Devon, I took him to see the room and he wanted it for her. It was a beautiful room; light and airy, and he knew she would be happy in it. He decided to take the room. This is just what he wanted for his wife. Not only that, but it was also just around the corner from where he lived. It would be good for him too, knowing she was not too far away from him.

Now, a place had been found for her to move into, they released her from the hospital, and I took her to her new home. I went to the hospital to pick her up. I had dropped her husband off at the nursing home with her personal belongings. He would get the place ready for her to move into.

Travelling to Burghfield Common from the hospital, my adoptive mum was chatting to me. Out of the blue she said to me, "You will take care of my husband for me, won't you?"

I said to her, "Of course I will. As much as he will allow me to. I do not want to tread in places with him he does not want me to go."

She then proceeded to say to me, "Thank you for everything you have done for me Avril, I will never forget what you have done for me." And she told me how much she loved me.

It was a strange conversation we'd had. We chatted happily together as I was driving her to her new home at the nursing home. When we got there her husband was already inside her room getting things ready for her to move in. She loved her room. They hugged one another and she seemed really happy.

We went every day to see her, and we took my daughter with us when we could. My adoptive mum loved my daughter so much and she was so happy when she did see her.

My adoptive Mum had been in the home just two weeks when disaster struck. I had taken her husband for his weekly shop, and on the way home we decided to pop into the home. When we got there, the staff told us they had to phone up to get the doctor to come and see his wife, as she was unwell. After hearing the news from the staff, we went straight to her room to see her. She certainly did look unwell.

We talked to her for a while trying to comfort her, but this did not do any good. I was praying for her and hoped the doctor would come soon.

In the meantime, because we had done the shopping, we thought the best thing to do was drop him back at home, and come back to the home whilst he put his shopping away. He needed some space.

I went back to the nursing home and was greeted by the doctor. He told me I had missed her by minutes, she had just died. I was in total shock. I went into her room to see her.

The staff tried to comfort me. Now I had the hard task of telling my adoptive dad that his wife had died. I told him what the nursing home had told me, and we both cried together. We were both devastated at this sad news.

When I left him, he got in touch with his family in Devon. Both of his nieces came to be with him. I felt I had to take a step back and let them have their time together. I had to leave them to adjust to the fact that his wife and their aunty was gone.

I told my husband and daughter the sad news. The doctor and nursing home had done all they could for her. Her time had come. When I looked back at everything that had taken place, I believe she knew her time was coming, this is why she thanked me and asked me to take care of her husband.

I helped my adoptive dad to gather everything he needed to get the funeral together. He chose Walkers Funeral Directors in Reading to do the funeral. We notified his nieces and kept praying for them, keeping them updated with the progress we were making.

This all took place in October 1996.

Chapter 28

The Enemy

2 Thessalonians 3:3 NIV The Lord is faithful, and He will strengthen you and protect you from the evil one.

The day had arrived for my adoptive mum's funeral to take place, at Henley Road Cemetery, Reading.

My adoptive dad's nieces had arrived, and I took a back seat as they were family.

The day was an amazing day. It was like heaven had come down to earth, and Jesus was with us through the whole service. The minister who took the service was filled full of the Holy Spirit of God, and everything went as planned. I had never been to such a glorious funeral. God was in the midst of His people that day. At least I knew she was with Jesus, this helped me in my grieving.

After the ceremony we went back to my adoptive dad's place for something to eat. His nieces took control of the situation. It was nice what they had done for him.

Finally, it was time for them to return to Devon. I told them they had no need to be worried as I would continue to look after their uncle, and I would keep them updated about how he was doing. They left happily knowing I would take care of him.

I decided I was going to get another job. The work I had done with my adoptive parents was done. I applied for a position at the Hollies Nursing Home, where my adoptive mum spent her last days. The position I applied for was an administrative role, working for the matron.

I was interviewed for the job, and it was mine. I thought, by working at the home, I could do some good in helping those less fortunate than myself. It was part-time work, and it fitted in nicely with my home life and also with looking after my adoptive dad.

I began my new job on Monday 18 November 1996. The matron greeted me and introduced me to other members of the staff who worked there. The first day I thought had gone well. I finished doing my work then went home to my husband and told him how my day went. I told my husband I would pick our daughter up from school but would go and see my adoptive dad first, to tell him how my day went.

We shared a lovely time together. I told him about the job I had started, and he seemed happy for me and also because I had taken a job where his wife had been. In a strange way, the job I was doing brought comfort to us both.

Eventually, it was time for me to leave him and pick my daughter up from school. We said our goodbyes to one another, and he waved to me as I left his place.

There was a lorry parked on the grass in front of his flat. I had parked my car on the road. I was careful as I maneuvered myself around the lorry to get into my car. I was particularly careful that afternoon because of what I believed God had spoken to me in the morning. He told me the enemy would trip me up, but He would be there to catch me.

I put my car key into my car door, when all of a sudden my ankle gave way, and I began falling. I cried out, "Satan I come against you in the name of Jesus Christ!" And I was on the ground.

I was unable to move or get up. I shouted out to my adoptive dad to tell him to call my husband to tell him what had happened to me. I felt awful; this was the last thing he needed at this time. I tried to get up, but was unable to do so. My leg was in a strange position.

My husband came straight to me where he could see me on the ground. He went into my adoptive dad's flat and phoned for an ambulance.

Our next-door neighbour was passing and asked my husband if he could do anything to help us. My husband and neighbour made me as comfortable as they could, and then our neighbour told my husband he would pick our daughter up from school and take her to his house where he and his wife would look after her until we got home from the hospital.

We were waiting for the ambulance to arrive. It was really cold on the floor, but I had to wait, as the ambulance had been detoured to another case. I waited there for some time, and was really cold, even though my husband tried to keep me warm.

The 18 November 1996 is a day I would not forget in a hurry. God's words came true. The enemy had tripped me up, but God was there to catch me.

The ambulance finally arrived. The paramedics examined me and told me that they had to straighten my leg out. They gave me gas and air so they could do the procedure they needed to do. Then they got me into the ambulance, and I was on the way to hospital. My husband followed the ambulance in his car so we would have transport to come home in.

The paramedics took me into the emergency department where I was put into a side room to be assessed. I was in hospital for a number of hours, and they had to draw off blood from my kneecap as it was badly swollen. They put an elastic stocking on my knee, and told me to come back the next day where they would look further into my situation. I was given crutches and told not to bear any weight on my leg. The hospital gave me strong pain killers to help with the pain.

My husband got me into the car, and we made our way home. He just stopped at our neighbours' to pick up our daughter.

When we arrived home, it was difficult for me to get upstairs, so when I eventually did get upstairs, I stayed there until I had to go to the hospital the next day. My husband had to do everything for my daughter and myself.

I had numerous appointments at the hospital. They put my leg into a leg-brace, but that didn't work, so they put my leg into plaster. They wanted the swelling to come down, but this was taking time. I was not allowed to bear weight on the leg for some time.

When the plaster was taken off, the hospital wanted to do an MRI scan, to look more closely at the knee. The MRI scan showed meniscal (cartilage) tears, and ACL (Anterior Cruciate Ligament) tears with instability in the knee. I had to have an operation to try and fix my leg.

The consultant cleaned my knee out from the debris they found inside, and the hospital hoped this would help my leg to heal.

The consultant told me if I had any problems with the 'disability process', I was to tell them to get in touch with him. I hadn't realised I was disabled and could claim disability. Because of this accident, I was registered disabled. I had to give my job up due to my condition. All in all, I only worked at the Hollies Nursing Home for half a day.

I also had to employ a cleaner to do the housework I was unable to do. I had no option but to ask for the help I needed. I found this experience very humbling. I employed her to come and clean for me once a week and I coped with the rest of the things I needed to do. It was a struggle, but with God's help I did what I needed to do.

The hospital referred me to the pain clinic because of the pain I was still in. I appreciated everything the hospital tried to do for me, but after a number of years on crutches, my husband thought I should get a second opinion. We had a private consultation with a consultant at the Hampshire Clinic in Old Basing. My husband was concerned that my leg was not getting any better. He thought if we had a second opinion, maybe something could be done.

I saw the consultant and he examined me thoroughly. He said to me, "Mrs. English, this would cost you a fortune if I did this privately, but I'll tell you what I am going to do for you, I am going to do everything you need on the NHS." Wow, I was shocked at what God had done. He was going to do everything for me - all the tests I needed - on the NHS. I had another arthroscopy operation, and the surgeon did all the tests he promised to do on the NHS. Finally, a firm diagnosis was given to me.

I was referred to the physiotherapy department, where they assigned me exercises, and told me I would have to go into the hydrotherapy pool to do the exercises they had given me.

This really helped me to build up the muscle which had wasted away in my leg. When my time was finished at their hydrotherapy pool, they gave me a list of further pools I could attend, where the pool was the right temperature for my leg.

The swimming pool which was most suitable for me was at the Apollo Hotel in Basingstoke. I could go to the swimming pool as often as I liked, and so I went three times a week. I was still on crutches but felt my leg was better than it was.

God does not do things by half. If He says He is going to do something for you, all you have to do is put your love, faith, trust and confidence in Him, take your hands off the situation and leave all of the consequences to Him. He is such a faithful God; He will always fulfil the promises He makes. All He wants is our trust and faith and have confidence in Him to help you in your need. God has been faithful to me, and I was so grateful and thankful to Him for His faithfulness to me.

He helped me to cope with my disability. I was still on crutches, but swimming and doing regular exercises in the pool helped me to cope with my condition, my leg became easier and I was able to manage, with God's help.

Chapter 29

New Car

Joshua 21:45 NIV Not one of all the Lord's good promises to Israel failed, every one was fulfilled.

One day whilst I was praying, the Lord said to me, "Avril, I am going to bring you a brand-new car." I just thanked God in faith. If God wanted to give me a new car, I knew without a shadow of a doubt He would do this for me. It was God's business not mine. I was not in a position to buy a new car, so I relied upon God to do this for me.

God made it possible for me to have a new car in the most amazing way. I received a letter about disability, and how I could claim disability allowance. I had been awarded disability living allowance at the high rate, which enabled me to go through the Motability scheme to get a new car. Moreover, I qualified to have a new car every three years.

At least I could put the disability allowance to good use; having this car enabled me to get around more easily, and to have a better quality of life than if I didn't have a car.

I could not believe the way God had done this. I did not like being disabled, but I was grateful and thankful to God that He was going to make it a lot easier for me to cope with my disability. I could not drive a manual car because of my disability, but because I qualified for the Motability Scheme I could get a brand-new automatic car, which would make driving easy for me.

All I had to do was put petrol in the car, the disability scheme took care of the rest. My husband was allowed to drive my car, but I had to be in the car when he drove it.

God in His faithfulness had done something amazing for me. It would never have entered my head to claim disability, but He made it possible for me to do this. God wanted me to trust Him no matter what my circumstances would be. He showed me through this accident how faithful He has been to me. God continued to make me grow in faith in my walk with Him. I could constantly see God answering the prayers I petitioned to Him. I knew that no matter what I prayed, God would answer me in accordance with His will. My faith was being made stronger each day.

Although God constantly tested my faith to prove it was genuine, He did this to grow me up in faith. He was building my faith on the rock and foundation of Christ. The more I studied the Bible and prayed, the better I knew my God. I leaned upon, relied upon, and depended upon Him to meet all my needs.

Chapter 30

Adoptive Dad Moves Away

Jeremiah 29:14 NIV "I will gather you from all the nations and places where I have banished you, declares the Lord, and will bring you back to the place from which I carried you into exile."

I was getting concerned for my adoptive dad's welfare. I was not able to look after him the way I did before, because of my disability. I was on crutches and having difficulty walking. I hobbled down the road to see him when I could, and I asked my friend to help him with his weekly shop, but it was not the same as it was when I did everything I could for him. It was time for me to admit I was not in the same place I was when his wife was alive. I wasn't able to do the things the way I used to for him before I had my accident. It was time for me to phone his family in Devon and tell them the situation I was in. We discussed what we could do to give their uncle the best quality of life. Then his niece told me that a house had just become available two doors down from a friend of his lived in Devon. She told me to leave it with her to see if she could get this house secured for him. At least he would have his family near him. She would be just down the road, so she would be able to pop in daily to see her uncle.

So, I left it with her. Obviously, his nieces talked with him about him moving back to Ashreigney, Chulmleigh, in Devon. He wanted to live next to his friend and family in the village he knew well.

I had been praying and praying about his situation. The last thing I'd wanted was for him to move away, but I wanted what was right and best for him.

God was so good to me. Within two weeks of my conversation with his family, his nieces had secured the house in the street where his friend and family lived. He would vacate his flat and move into his new home.

My prayer partner and I helped him with the moving preparations. It was a miracle of God that his move had come about so quickly.

It was coming to the end of the year 1999 when the time came to move my adoptive dad to Devon. We made all the necessary arrangements. On the day of the move, our daughter would stay with a friend for the afternoon after school until we returned. My husband asked his son if he wouldn't mind helping him move our adoptive dad's belongings. His son agreed to help him do this.

On moving day, my husband rented a van, and his son and he packed the van up with all our adoptive dad's belongings, and they drove to Devon. I took my car and drove our adoptive dad to his new home. His nieces were getting his new place ready for him to move into. They were waiting for their uncle and his furniture to arrive.

We had a good journey to Devon, and before we knew it, we had arrived at my adoptive dad's new home. My husband, his son and my adoptive dad's nieces unloaded everything from the van, and we did all that we could to make a lovely home for our adoptive dad.

His nieces unpacked the boxes and put his things away. Their uncle gave me a tour of his new home, he looked so happy and pleased to be moving into his new home.

The house was really big and spacious, the only thing that was missing was gas central heating – instead there was an open fire, which would do the job of heating the radiators to keep his place warm. This didn't seem to bother him. Before long, everything was unpacked and put away. My adoptive dad's new home was ready for him to enjoy. After we chatted for a little while with his family, it was time for us to leave and go home to Burghfield Common.

My husband and his son drove the rented van back to the place where they hired it from. I followed behind them in my car. We arrived back in Burghfield Common and picked our daughter up from her friend's.

It seemed so strange not having my adoptive dad living down the road from me, and not be able to pop in to see him. I had to accept this, but at times it was hard for me to grasp.

We phoned one another regularly. I was glad to hear he was settling into his home nicely. He seemed to be very happy living where he was living. I missed him so much, but I had to accept that this was God's will for him. I was not in the place to do things for him as I used to.

Life continued on, until at the beginning of February 2000, I received a phone call from his niece. She told me I was not to worry, but that she had called in to see her uncle, and found him on the floor. She had called an ambulance, and the medical staff had taken him into hospital.

They diagnosed him with hypothermia. He had gone downstairs in the night to put coal on the fire and fell down. He did not put the coal on the fire, and he wasn't near the phone. He was unable to call his niece. When she found him, he had been on the floor all night. They kept him in hospital, and he told his niece not to let me come to Devon, as he was okay.

The next day I was getting my daughter ready for school when the phone rang. It was my adoptive dad's niece phoning me to tell me that her uncle had died in the early hours of the morning. This news hit me hard. He had been back in Devon for just six weeks, now he had died.

God knew the plans He had made for him. He wanted him back home with his nieces, who were able to care for him better than I could. My family were devastated at the news, but we had to remember he was in the place God had wanted him to be. If he had lived in Burghfield Common, it would have made it harder for his nieces to take care of him, and now the funeral arrangements, and to settle his affairs, so God's plans were that he could be taken care of in the right way. He made sure the details were in place so that he could end his days with the girls.

They were all so happy together, and even though it was only six weeks they shared together, they had made the most of the time.

My adoptive dad died on the 8th of February 2000. Now he was with his wife once again. This brought comfort to my heart.

Chapter 31

New House

2 Samuel 7:27-29 NIV "Lord Almighty, God of Israel, You have revealed this to Your servant, saying, 'I will build a house for you.' So Your servant has found courage to pray this prayer to you.

Sovereign Lord, You are God! Your covenant is trustworthy, and You have promised these good things to Your servant. Now be pleased to bless the house of Your servant, that I may continue forever in Your sight; for You, Sovereign Lord, You have spoken, and with Your blessing the house of Your servant will be blessed forever."

I had a desire within my heart we should move from the house we were living in. I just kept praying and praying over the whole situation. I'd felt I had confirmation to move when God led me to the Scripture:

Genesis 12:1-4 NIV The Lord said to Abram, Go from your country, your people and your father's household to the land I will show you. I will make your name great, and you will be a blessing. I will bless those who bless you, and whoever curses you I will curse; and all peoples on earth will be blessed through you. So Abram went, as the Lord had told him, and Lot went with him. Abram was seventy-five years old when he set out from Harran.

We had booked a holiday to Florida, in America. We were taking one of my daughter's friends with us. Everything was on track for us to go away when I became sick. I made an appointment with the doctor. After he examined me, he advised me not to go on holiday because my illness was a recurring illness, and the insurance company would not insure me. So, I had to go home and tell my husband I was unable to go. My husband was not at all pleased. He thought I still should go regardless of what the doctor had said. I had to dig my heels in and tell him I was unable to go. I had to take the advice of my GP. I could not risk going to America feeling as I did.

My husband was not going to cancel the holiday. He was still going to take my daughter and her friend to Florida. At the time this was happening I felt angry, frustrated, and very hurt that he was going to do this and leave me behind. He told me that he did not want to lose the money he had paid out for us to go on holiday, so he decided he would take the girls away and I would have to stay at home. I felt unloved, rejected, and very, very, hurt. My mind was doing overtime. I felt rebellious towards him, and thought to myself I would not be in the house when he returned home.

On the Tuesday, before he was going to go on holiday on the Saturday, he came home from work suggesting he wanted to put our house on the market. I listened to what he was saying. I had been praying about a move for a while, but I kept this to myself. He said he was going to get three estate agents in to value the house. I had prayed and asked God whether this was His will. I continued to pray over the whole situation. I asked God that if this was His will we sell the house that He would bring the right price with the right buyer, and that he would sell the house swiftly and quickly.

So, my husband did what he said he was going to do, and the estate agents came. We chose the one we wanted to put the house on the market with. My husband, daughter and her friend left on the Saturday to go on holiday. Our house was on the market, and I waited for the estate agent to get in touch with me to bring the people who wanted to view the house. God obviously had a plan; this is why He did not want me to go to America. He used my sickness so that I could stay at home and be there to sell the house. It was a lot easier for me to cope with keeping the house tidy and clean whilst my family was away. It made the viewings easier for me.

My family had been gone a couple of days when I told my husband we had an offer on the house. The couple were really keen to buy our property. I asked my husband what he wanted me to do. He said, "Agree to the sale, but on the understanding the couple will have to wait until we have found a property to buy." So, I did what my husband suggested. The house was under offer.

I was led to a new housing development in Basingstoke. I felt God was leading me to go and look at the houses. God knew if we were going to live there. If so, He already had reserved a house for us. I continued to trust Him to guide and lead me into His perfect will.

I saw a house on the front of the development near a road. I liked the house, so I sent the details to my husband. I was keeping him in the loop with what was happening.

Unfortunately, someone else bought the first property I liked. The developer came back to me with another plot, which she said was much better than the plot I was going for. It was going to be ready in the September. It was lovely plot, better than the first house I liked. I felt this was the house God wanted us to have.

I had to test it, so I sent all the details via email to America, and asked my husband what he wanted me to do. He told me to tell the developer that we would put a deposit on the plot, and when he came home from America he would come and view the plot.

I did not want to sway my husband in any way, we both would have to be on the same page. I continued to pray about the whole situation. My husband came home from holiday, we went to see the plot with our daughter, and we decided that we would go for it and buy the property.

It was a beautiful house, a four-bedroom detached, with two ensuites to the two main bedrooms, and a family bathroom. Downstairs, there was a utility room, kitchen-diner, dining room, study, lounge and a downstairs cloakroom. It had a nicely sized garden out the back, and the front of the house was a good size too with potential to make the front garden beautiful. There was a double garage and a piece of land to the side of the garage with enough space to park a caravan. All-in-all there was enough space to park seven cars around the front of the house!

I asked God for confirmation that this was His will, and the confirmation came. The name of the road was Priest Down.

When all the legal paperwork was complete, we moved into our new home on the 28 September 2001. My husband named the house, 'Pastures New'.

It never ceased to amaze me, what God was doing in our lives. I never thought in a million years we would be able to move into a house like this.

This was an exciting adventure we were on, and I was living it in the centre of God's will. I just wondered what God going to do next…

Chapter 32

Driving Lessons

We bought our daughter her first car, a Ford KA. We booked driving lessons and put her through an intensive driving course. After she passed her test, we put her through an advanced course, because this made the insurance for her car cheaper. We were so proud of her.

Whilst she was learning to drive, to give her extra practice, she would drive me to her school in the mornings, and after school, she drove me home again.

She had to take the driving test twice, but on her second attempt she passed with flying colours.

This gave our daughter more independence. She was now able to meet her friends, and I did not have to drive her everywhere she wanted to go.

After she finished her education in Burghfield Common, our daughter went to the University of Southampton to do a maths and computer science degree.

Halfway through the course, she dropped the computer science part as she found it too much on top of her mathematics degree. She did very well, and we helped in any way we could. She loved studying there and had met and made many new friends.

She got her mathematics degree and took a year out, working for a firm in Basingstoke to save up to do her master's degree. She did not want her dad and I to pay for this degree, as we had paid for her first one. She applied to Southampton University to take her master's degree there, and she successfully completed the course.

Chapter 33

Moving Again

Genesis 12:1 NIV The Lord said to Abram, "Go from your country, your people and your father's household to the land I will show you."

God wanted us to move from Basingstoke and back into the area near to my husband's work. The commute was getting more difficult for him due to the heavy traffic. We decided to put the house onto the market and sell. We found the estate agents who would market our house for us, and we were on the move again.

It did not take long for a buyer to come and to offer us a good price for our house. It was immaculate and the buyers fell in love with it.

They wanted us to vacate the property on the 13th of December 2007, which we agreed to do. We found a house to buy, and the sale was going through.

However, the week before we were due to move, the current owners of the house we were buying told us that the property they wanted to buy was in probate and wasn't ready. Since we needed to vacate our house on the agreed date, we decided that we would find rented accommodation, rather than let our buyers down.

Just one day before our move, we found a place to rent at Three Mile Cross. We had to tell the removals company to take our things to the new address. At least we had somewhere to live.

We made an agreement to rent for six months. This would give us the time we needed to find somewhere else to live, as we would no longer go through with the house we had planned to buy.

Christmas was coming up, so we decided to leave it until after Christmas before we looked again for a house to buy. We put our name down on the estate agents' list and then after Christmas we began to look.

Shortly afterwards, our doctors in the new location sent me to have a mammogram at the Reading Hospital. The results were in, and it was clear.

A few months later, in May 2008, we bought our new house. There was some work which needed doing before we could move in. My husband completed the work before we all moved in in June.

He built fitted wardrobes into two of the bedrooms and put a wardrobe into the third bedroom. We moved all our clothes over to the new house, so it was less for us to move when we moved in the June.

We needed to put a new kitchen in, so my husband ordered that and gave our old kitchen to his son, so as not to waste it.

We registered with the doctors in Mortimer. In July 2009, I was called by the doctors to go and have another mammogram. At first, I was not going to go as I'd just had one the year before, and because it was clear I did not think there was a need for me to go again. My husband, however, was persistent that I should go, so I went and had it done in the mobile unit in Mortimer.

Well, the results came in and I was called to go to Berkshire Radiology to discuss my results. I knew immediately things were not good. I prayed to the Lord, and I asked Him, "Lord, have I got Cancer?"

His response to me was, 'Yes'.

The day of the appointment had arrived. My husband came with me to the hospital. In the waiting room I was constantly praying to God. My name was called, and I was asked to go into a room where the doctor was waiting for me. The doctor's computer was on and there was something on the screen, but I did not take any notice of it. The doctor began to talk to my husband and me about the mammogram. He told us they had found breast cancer. I was not shocked by this news, simply because I prayed to God, and I felt that He had given me the answer to the question when I had asked Him. So, for me this was the confirmation I had been waiting for from God.

The doctor told me he was going to do a biopsy, and my husband was told to leave the room. A nurse attended the procedure and the doctor did the biopsy. When this was done the nurse called my husband back into the room. We were told I would have to go and see the breast clinic nurse. She would go through the procedure with me, and she would be the one who would be looking after me. The nurse told me that the doctor was sending my biopsy away to be tested. I would have an appointment with the consultant in urology, and he would deal with the cancer.

The nurse addressed my husband and told him that he would have to let me do things the way I wanted them to be done. I had the information I needed, and the appointment came to an end.

My husband and I left radiology, and we walked back to our car. I could see my husband did not believe what the doctor and nurse had said. He did not want to discuss the situation with me.

I wanted to go to Southampton and tell our daughter face to face and tell her the outcome of my appointment. My husband was in denial and did not want to go to Southampton. He kept saying he wanted to wait to see what the results of the biopsy are, even though the mammogram showed I had cancer.

Later that evening we had a phone call from our daughter asking me how things went at the hospital. I began to talk to her and told the truth about what the hospital had said. She burst into tears, and when my husband heard she was in tears, he then also burst into tears. In fact, all of us were in tears. I did all I could to try and comfort her and tell her everything would be okay. I did not want her to worry or be anxious about me as she was in the middle of her master's degree. My daughter told me she would come home from university to help me.

My appointment came through to see the consultant. The consultant confirmed I did have breast cancer, and it was malignant. The surgeon was going to do a lumpectomy, and remove lymph nodes from under my arm to make sure the cancer had not spread into the lymph nodes. I continued to praise and thank God for all His faithfulness to me. If I had not had the mammogram in Mortimer, I would never have known I had cancer. God knew I had cancer, even before I knew I had it. This is why He made my husband insistent that I go and have the mammogram. To be truthful if my husband hadn't been insistent, I would not have gone.

I believe God moved us back into Burghfield Common, so that I would be able to attend the Royal Berkshire Hospital to have the operation. I also would be able to have follow-up treatment at the hospital. God was so good to me, and I could not thank Him and praise Him enough for His love and faithfulness to me.

The operation took place on 21 August 2009. My daughter came home from Southampton University. The university had given her compassionate leave and she could do her work from home. After a number of weeks after the operation had taken place, my treatment began. I had radiotherapy treatment every weekday for a month. When I went to see the consultant for my follow up appointment he put me on Tamoxifen. He told me I would be on this drug for five years.

All I can say about this, is that I was so pleased God had prepared me for what was ahead. He has always been faithful to me, and without Him I would not have been able to go through what I had been through. A friend of mine gave me this Scripture:

Isaiah 38:5 NIV This is what the Lord, the God of your father David says: I have heard your prayer and seen your tears; I will add fifteen years to your life.

The Word of God gave me strength and courage. If I had negative thoughts, I would remember what God had said to me through His Word, and this drove out all negativity because I put my trust in Him.

Wow! What a great and awesome God I had. He made sure the cancer would not be hidden, and He brought the darkness into the light of His eternal kingdom. Once again, He saved my life in love and faithfulness, I could never thank Him enough.

Heavenly Father, thank You for bringing me back from captivity. Thank You that You have gathered us from the nations and places when I believed in You, and You brought me back to the place You exiled me from. In the precious name of Jesus Christ. Amen

Chapter 34
Marriage Proposal

Genesis 2:24 NIV That's why a man leaves his father and mother and is united to his wife, and they become one flesh.

I had been praying about my daughter for many years. I wanted her to be in the will of God when she got married. Every boyfriend she had, I prayed individually about them and asked God that, if they were the not the one He wanted her to marry, then He would remove them. It was so important to me that she married the person God had planned for her.

2 Corinthians 6:14 NIV Do not be yoked together with unbelievers. For what do righteousness and wickedness have in common?

When I married my husband, neither of us had a personal relationship with Jesus Christ. When I did become a Christian, I wanted my husband to have a relationship with Jesus Christ and know the glory of God, as I had done. I have come to understand the decision is not mine to make. Each individual person has to choose for themselves whether he/she wants to be a follower of Jesus Christ. The decision is between them and God.

The salvation of the Lord belongs to God and certainly not to me. No one has a right to push Christianity onto another person. God only requires me to pray for my husband and child and leave all the consequences to Him. He knows who His children are.

My daughter, when she was younger, had made a commitment to God. She pleaded with me to be baptised in the Holy Spirit of God. I told her before I prayed for her what the commitment meant. I have never pushed my faith onto my husband or daughter, I have left them to choose what they wanted for their own lives.

At the age of three, my daughter had a divine encounter with God, she told me He had come to her bedside. She described to me what she had seen. When she was about to go into senior school at the age of eleven, she pleaded with me to ask God to fill her with the Holy Spirit of God.

She explained to me that she did not want a water baptism at this time, but she did want to be filled with the Holy Spirit of God. She seemed to understand what she was asking me to do, so I did pray for her to be filled full of the Holy Spirit of God. She prayed the sinner's prayer then I prayed and asked God to baptise her in the name of God the Father, and God the Son, and God the Holy Spirit. I prayed God to come into her heart and life and fill her with His love, grace, mercy, and peace. I prayed the Holy Spirit of God would fill her with His supernatural power from the top of her head to the tips of her toes. I praised and thanked God for her salvation and the commitment she had made to God. I constantly prayed daily for her that she would continue to follow Him.

I tried to live my life being the example within the home. My husband and child knew who I stood for. I did not need to push my faith onto them or ram my faith constantly down their throats. They had to make their own decisions about faith, all God has called me to do is pray daily for them and I do just that.

When my daughter was studying for her master's degree, she took a job on campus. This is where she met her future husband. They got on well together and liked the same things. He was six years older than she was. Our daughter needed someone who was mature, as she was very mature herself. We had met him on a number of occasions, and we could see they were well matched.

When her boyfriend came to us ask for her hand in marriage, I was away visiting my brother in Darlington, Co. Durham. My husband did not give his consent straight away. He told her boyfriend that he would speak to me first then give his decision afterwards. I was so delighted that he had asked for our daughter's hand in marriage. I liked her boyfriend, and I knew that they loved one another so I told my husband to go ahead and tell him he could marry her.

Her boyfriend told us to keep it under wraps, as he wanted it to be a surprise for her. She had no idea about forthcoming proposal. So, we honoured his request.

They were at a music festival in Dorset with their friends when he proposed. Her boyfriend had it all planned out. He had a special wooden ring made for her to take to the festival, as he did not want to take the real one with him, just in case it was stolen. When he asked her to marry him, she burst into tears and said, 'Yes!'

So, he put the wooden ring on her finger. She was so thrilled. All their friends were so happy for them when they told them the news.

He had asked his best friend in Southampton to put a bouquet of flowers and a bottle of champagne in his flat, so that when they returned from the festival, he could ask her officially to marry him. They came back from the festival, and he presented her with a ring he'd had made for her; a palladium gold solitaire diamond ring.

As soon as he placed the real ring on her finger, she phoned us up to tell us the great news. Unbeknownst to her we already knew he was going to ask her to marry him.

Immediately, they came to Burghfield Common to show us her ring and celebrate with us. It was lovely to see them both so happy.

They were married at Highfield's Church in Southampton, on 28 April 2012.

After the wedding we went to their favourite restaurant, The Dock of the Bay in Southampton. The immediate family had a sit-down meal, and in the evening their friends joined the wedding party, and a buffet was put on for them all to enjoy.

It was such a special day. Everyone enjoyed it. I shall remember her wedding for the rest of my life, they were married in a Spirit-filled church where the minister of the church was a born-again Christian. All the prayers I had prayed for her over the years were answered that day.

Chapter 35

A House of Prayer

Psalm 45:1 NIV My heart is stirred by a noble theme as I recite my verses for the king. My tongue is the pen of a skilful writer.

My daughter and her husband were coming to stay overnight, so my husband could take them to Heathrow Airport, to fly to Antigua for their honeymoon.

Life continued on for me. I had done I what I believed God called me to do in raising our daughter. Now, I could focus on what God's plans were for my life. God had been encouraging me to write a book. Bit by bit, ideas were being revealed to me about what I should do. He had brought me the facilities I needed, as I could write it in the comfort of my armchair.

Isaiah 50:4 NIV The Sovereign Lord has given me a well-instructed tongue, to know the word that sustains the weary. He wakens me morning by morning, wakens my ear to listen like one being instructed.

I began to write what I believed God wanted me to write. I asked God each day to equip, empower, increase my faith to believe in Him that I could do this enormous task. He gave me the assurance and confidence I needed to write the book the way He wanted it done. God filled me with wisdom and knowledge and led me to the material I had written years earlier in my diaries. The book was to be called: 'A House of Prayer – Daily Devotional.'

I was not going to be distracted from doing this. Jesus Christ had transformed my life. I wanted to share with others the teachings and lessons God had blessed me with, through everything He had done in my life. Prayer was the most important lesson I had learned through the Holy Spirit of God. It completely changed my life, and it enabled me to have a great relationship with God. I did not want others to miss out or be ignorant of the truth as I had been. Now I could write prayers and lessons to help others in their everyday life, and hopefully help them learn what God can do for them if we allow Him to. I wanted them to make up their own minds whether it was true or not. This had to be their decision not mine.

It took me four months from the beginning to the end to write this book. My younger brother kindly offered to edit the book for me. On editing the book, my brother told me that the book was ministering to him. He told me through the book he became a Christian.

A friend of mine had sent me a gift of £1,000. I felt God was confirming He wanted me to get the book published. I was a complete novice in all of this, and I had no idea how I was going to do this task. I was in constant prayer asking God to show me how I was to do this step-by-step. He brought me a publisher's name. I got in touch with a number of publishers, but felt that I was being led by God to go with Author House, so this is what I did. 'A House of Prayer – Daily Devotional', was published in November 2012.

I was asked to speak on American radio and do a live broadcast about the book. I was really nervous doing this, but I had no other choice but to trust in the Lord, with all my heart, and lean not on my own understanding. In all my ways I acknowledged Him and He made my path clear and straight. The host on the radio show thought the interview went really well. He used the interview again the following week.

My daughter and son-in-law set up a website for me where the public could buy the book if they wanted to. I began a blog and posted it onto social media: Facebook, Twitter, and Google+ three times a week, so I felt that I was getting things out to the media. God once again remained faithful to me. He told me the book would be published. I have never given up believing that when God has told me He would do something within my life, He is faithful to do it. Time and time again He has proven His faithfulness to me.

Habakkuk 2:1-3 NIV I will look and see what He will say to me, and what answer I am to give to this complaint. Then the LORD replied: "Write down the revelation and make it plain on tablets so that a herald may run with it. For the revelation awaits an appointed time; it speaks of the end and will not prove false. Though it linger, wait for it; it will certainly come and not delay."

Chapter 36

A Miracle of God

Jeremiah 30:17 NIV I will restore you to health and heal your wounds, declares the Lord.

I received a phone call on 10 August 2013 from my nephew in Switzerland. He was absolutely distraught. His mum was taken to hospital by helicopter to a university hospital in Switzerland. My sister was critically ill. My sister's husband phoned my sister's friend and she came straight over to her. Immediately she gave her CPR (Cardiopulmonary Resuscitation) until the paramedics arrived. Her friend saved my sister's life, and I was really grateful to her for this.

The professor and his team were notified by the air ambulance and were waiting for my sister to arrive at the hospital. They rushed her into A&E where she was assessed, and then straight into the operating theatre where everything was prepared for the operation to take place. An aneurysm had burst in her brain, and she was in a critical condition.

The professor operated and dealt with the burst aneurysm, but there were also other aneurysms – one of which he dealt with, but one aneurysm was too difficult to get to and so they would have to leave that one for another time. They got my sister stable, and she was now in intensive care, where they were keeping a close eye on her.

I was praying constantly for her and also got a team of people who were intercessors to pray for her. I had to trust God in faith for a good outcome from the situation. My sister was dangerously ill, her life was in the balance and her whole situation was taken out of her hands and mine. I was in total shock and so was the rest of my family. At the time I really thought my sister's time had come.

My nephew kept me updated daily, I then passed on the progress she was making to the rest of the family. It was the power of prayer that comforted me at this time. I knew the only person who could deliver my sister through this dreadful ordeal was God alone. She was a committed Christian, so I knew God was with her. God had always been faithful to me in answering my prayers. I committed her into His hands and accepted that, whatever the outcome was going to be in my sister's life - God was completely in control.

Jeremiah 30:17 NIV I will restore you to health and heal your wounds, declares the Lord.

This Scripture sustained me over the dark days. I believed God would restore my sister to health and heal her wounds. The hospital wanted her to go Valence, a place in Switzerland where she could have all the right facilities to help her become stronger in her recovery. They wanted her to be there for a few months.

Her recovery was slow but it was positive. Each day she became stronger and eventually when the treatment had finished, they sent her home. My sister was a walking miracle, and I have Jesus Christ to thank for this. No matter what the situation looked like in the eyes of the world, I kept my eyes focused on God and the promises He had made me. She came through the operation and made a complete recovery.

Hebrews 12:2 NIV Fixing our eyes on Jesus, the pioneer and perfecter of our faith. For the joy set before Him, He endured the cross, scorning its shame and sat down at the right hand of the throne of God.

Job 1:12 NIV The Lord said to Satan, "Very well, then, everything he has is in your power, but on the man himself do not lay a finger."

The Word of God strengthens you in all situations as long as you trust in His Word. If we trust in the Lord Jesus Christ, lean, depend, rely upon Him through the Holy Spirit of God, and His supernatural power in faith, nothing can touch us unless God gives His permission. He will never let you down. My sister was healed just as God said He would do. I give Him all the glory, honour, praise, adoration, and love for all of His faithfulness He has shown towards us His people. God won the battle over my sister's life.

Chapter 37

Sent to Switzerland

Hebrews 13:20-21 NIV Now may the God of peace, who through the blood of eternal covenant brought back from the dead our Lord Jesus, the great Shepherd of the sheep, equip you with everything good for doing His will, and may He work in us what is pleasing to Him through Jesus Christ, to whom be glory for ever and ever. Amen

My sister had to go into hospital the following November to have the final aneurysm done. She phoned to ask me if I would be with her when she had this done. I told her I would have to pray about this before I made any commitment to her. In the meantime, I consulted God and asked him if He wanted me to go to Switzerland. I put a 'fleece' out and asked God to provide flights and accommodation for me. If He did this then I knew I was in God's will. It was not long after my prayer I received the answer to my prayer.

My nephew phoned me to tell me he was going to purchase an airline ticket for me to fly to Switzerland. He said, "It was important to him that I would be there with his mum." He also offered me his flat to stay in while his mum was in the hospital and in her recovery.

My nephew was a pilot and worked for Lufthansa, so he was able to buy flights cheaply. I discussed at length with him what I could do to help him and his mum. My nephew thought with me being a support to my sister, his mum would have a reason to come through her operation. Not only that he wanted me to be a support to him as well. He knew how close we were as sisters, and I was his godmother. My sister did not need any stress in her life, and I am afraid she did have stress with her husband.

The professor who did her previous aneurism operation told my sister on no uncertain terms was she to be stressed in anyway. This is why I believe she wanted me to be with her in Switzerland. Her husband was not allowed into the hospital. She needed to be relaxed and stress-free.

My nephew and I arranged that I would go out to Switzerland at the beginning of November 2014. I would spend a number of days with her at her home before she went into hospital. At least this time my sister's operation was not going to be an emergency. I stayed at her home until she went into hospital. When it was time for her to go into hospital my nephew picked us both up. I had taken my suitcase from her home, and after we got my sister settled into the hospital, my nephew was going to take me to his flat where I would be until I went home to England.

The day arrived for my sister's operation. The professor told us the time the operation would take place. My nephew and I were waiting for the phone call from the professor to say the operation was successful. Both of us were praying constantly, so when the phone call came, the Professor told us everything went well and we could have a short visit in ICU (Intensive Care Unit). My nephew thanked the professor for everything he had done, and then we both burst into tears with relief that the operation was over.

We both went into ICU, and my sister knew we were there. She got hold of my little finger and said to me, "Thank you Ave for being here with me." Day by day she was becoming stronger. I visited her each day. Then it was time for her to go to Rheinfelden to the 'Park Resort' in the next stage of her recovery. She would be in this resort for a number of weeks.

My nephew had to fly a lot, so whilst he was away I would take care of his cat. This cat was called Muffin, and he had 'adopted' my nephew. The cat would come round to see my nephew for his food. While my nephew was away, Muffin would come and meow at the door until he got my attention. I thought it was funny that God had allowed me into this situation. He knew I was absolutely terrified of cats. This was God's cure for me – looking after this cat helped me to overcome the spirit of fear.

It was so strange having Muffin come daily, and sometimes he would stay overnight. This helped me to get over my fear of cats, and now I loved him. Muffin would come and sit on my lap to get my attention. At least I had a bit of company whilst my sister and nephew were away.

I had been in Switzerland for nearly a month. I was so grateful and thankful to God for the prayers and petitions He had answered for my sister. His Word truly had come to pass in Jeremiah 30:17, the Word God gave to me when she had her first aneurisms. He did restore my sister's health and He healed her wounds. God had healed my sister in an awesome way. Praying Scripture over her daily gave me strength and hope. God had granted me another miracle for her through the name of Jesus Christ.

I have an amazing and faithful God. He has never let me down. When I put my confidence in Him and not in my own ability and strength, He works His wonders. I trust Him in faith, and have the confidence to know when God speaks a Word of Promise, He will never let me down. I want to do things in the ways of Christ and have Him right in the centre of my heart and life. This is the best way I know how to do things.

Chapter 38

Abandon

2 Corinthians 4:9-11 NIV Persecuted, but not abandoned, struck down but not destroyed. We always carry around in our body the death of Jesus, so that that the life of Jesus may also be revealed in our body. For we, who are alive are always being given over to death for Jesus' sake, so that His life may also be revealed in our mortal body.

My elder brother was having a real hard time. He became a Christian in January 1990. The trouble was that when he became a Christian, he would evangelise to people, then tell them to ring me up so I could pray for them. I did this for a time then I felt the Lord say to me, "Avril, let your brother pray for the people he meets and don't do the praying for him." So, the next time my brother rang me requesting that I pray for a particular person, I told him he was quite capable of praying for the person himself. My brother took umbrage over this as he thought he couldn't pray. God was going to teach him how to pray, and was taking him out of his comfort zone. The was the beginning of my brother's prayer life.

When my brother returned home from Essex, his wife and family could see a dramatic change in my brother's life. His wife was a Muslim, but she did not practise her Muslim faith. She really did give her husband a hard time. They had two daughters who were married and had children. His wife was a very strong character and she did not listen to anything her husband said to her. She did everything she could do to quench my brother's faith in Jesus Christ. My brother constantly tried to tell her about Jesus Christ, but she was having none of it.

In the end, God took everything out of my brother's hands. His wife decided to put all his possessions into bin liners and throw him out of the house and onto the street. He was homeless. All because she could not control him or his faith in Jesus Christ.

His younger daughter and granddaughter took him in until my brother found a place to live. Eventually, after much prayer, God provided a place for my brother to live in. He qualified for a bungalow in sheltered accommodation in Darlington. This gave him back his independence and he began to know peace once again.

My brother divorced his wife because of her unreasonable behaviour. His wife had no grounds at all to divorce him. His divorce was granted in my brother's favour. His barrister told my brother to stay well clear of his ex-wife, as she was nothing but trouble. He had a horrendous time living with her and also a hard time away from her. My brother was a kind, loyal, and generous man (to a fault) and his family had always taken advantage of him.

My brother was living in a beautiful place, this was when his younger daughter asked him to be a caretaker for her home, as she was moving to Guildford to be with her daughter when she attended the ACM (The Academy of Contemporary Music). She had left the NHS as a nurse, and she had got new position in Guildford in Surrey, to be near her daughter as she attended the Academy.

This meant he would have to give up his sheltered accommodation. I felt he should not do this, but he did not listen to me. I felt my niece was using him for her own selfish gains. Knowing the family the way I did, I really did feel that he should not give up his bungalow for her. I tried to tell my brother not to do this, but he thought that he would be helping her. She persuaded him to look after her place and so I could do nothing about this.

So, he gave up his bungalow to take care of her property. His daughter was alright with her dad all the time he was taking care of her property.

When he had a big win on the horses, he even gave the money to her, and only stipulated that she had to give a small sum of the money to her uncle in America. She came home each weekend to sort out things she needed to sort out. Her daughter would always come home with her so she could see her grandad.

I constantly received calls from my niece about her problems. She told me she was unsettled in her workplace, and her daughter had nearly finished her education at Guildford.

Things began to change when my brother had a stroke. I could see that she did not want to look after him and she was becoming very intense about her situation.

This gave her opportunity she was looking for. She and her daughter came home from Surrey. Her daughter was going to finish the last of her education at home. My niece had handed in her notice from her present employment. She was already writing books with a friend of hers. It was her friend that suggested she begin a business at home. She got my great niece to do the same. She had enough money to live on as she had a big lump sum my brother had given to her.

I was constantly receiving texts and phone calls from my niece informing me of stories about my brother. Because I was a Christian, I felt unable to tell my brother what she was doing… She was putting me into situations whereby I could not betray her confidences, nor did I want to pour fuel onto the fire by telling my brother what she was doing, so I had to keep everything to myself. I prayed and asked God for wisdom how to handle it all.

When my niece revealed to me she was booking a holiday for her dad and mum to go to Portugal for a holiday together, my alarm bells began to ring.

She told me she needed a break from them both, so she could have respite for herself. I tried to be subtle and tell my brother not to go on holiday with his ex-wife, but once again he did not listen to me. So, I had to take my hands off the situation and I said no more to him, but I was in prayer for him.

Whilst my brother was in Portugal he phoned me up and told me he was having aggravation from his ex-wife. I wasn't at all surprised at the conversation we were having as this was one of the reasons why he divorced her. He was anxious and stressed out and all I could do was pray for him that the Lord would resolve this situation. It was not long before my prayer was answered.

My niece telephoned me to tell me the hospital in Portugal had rung her up informing her that her dad had a second stoke. She was blaming the stoke on her mother, telling me her mother was controlling, stressful, and wanted her own way in all things.

She was trying to convince herself that it was her mum who had caused the stroke, but in actual fact, she had a role to play in this situation. She was the one who had arranged the holiday for them both, knowing full well her mum would provoke arguments with her dad. She wanted what she wanted, now she had the consequences of her actions. She continued to tell me the doctors would not allow my brother to fly home until he was well enough. All I said to my niece was all I could do was pray to God about the whole situation and leave the consequences to Him. This was God's business not mine.

The next thing I heard, my niece had had enough of my brother living with her. She arranged an incident whereby she could get him to leave her house. It seemed she had finished having use for him.

I found it hard to hear that she had thrown my brother out of her house. He had left without his drugs or any clothes. He left with the clothes on his back and that was it. I knew she wanted rid of him but did not think she would go to the lengths she had done to get her own way. What hit me the most was she was a nurse, yet she could not allow my brother to have his medication or clothes? She knew my brother needed his medication.

Once again my brother was homeless, only this time it was worse than what happened previously when his ex-wife had thrown him out. The council gave him temporary accommodation until they found a place for him to live in permanently. My brother had friends from the Salvation Army, who were the ones who helped him. He needed to go back to his daughter's house to get his medication. They went with him and knocked on the door. His granddaughter answered the door, only after she had phoned her mum, and her mum had phoned the police.

The police arrived at her property. They asked my brother what he was doing there, and he explained to the police the reason why he was there. He needed his medication. When the police knew the real reason for him being there, they were the ones who knocked on the door. His granddaughter had no option but to answer the door to the police and they asked her to get his medication. This time it had all backfired on his daughter and granddaughter. They were trying to tell the police that he was harassing them. When he got his medication, he left.

When his friends from the Salvation Army saw the situation my brother was living in, they immediately offered him temporary accommodation. One of his friends from the Salvation Army helped my brother to get the right accommodation which would meet his needs.

These people were absolutely amazing to him. Once again God in His faithfulness was answering petitions on my brother's behalf. My brother's life began to change. God had put the right people in his path who were true Christians. Even though one of his friends was going through treatment for lung cancer, he was still there to give my brother the help he needed. The wife of this friend found a flat my brother could rent, which was warden-controlled. It was just around the corner from where they were living. They thought this accommodation was right for him as they would be able to keep an eye out for him.

My brother was allocated a flat, but he had to wait for the flat to become vacant. In the meantime, his friends continued to look after him until his flat would be ready to move into.

His daughter had made arrangements for my brother to pick up his things from her home. She gave him a time and date, and put his things into the garage at the time she stated. She did not want him on her property again.

His friends gathered together to go with him and make sure his daughter did not make any accusations against him anymore. His friends had hired a van for him and they were going to put the things he had at her place into storage until he was able to move into his flat. They picked up his things on the day his daughter wanted and moved everything out of her property.

My brother got the news that the flat that he was going to rent was now available for him to move into. The friends that he was living with got a team together and cleaned the flat from top to bottom. They got someone to come in to decorate the flat to make it fresh and clean but what amazed me was they also paid to have the decorating to be done. God had provided everything my brother needed through His people. Now he had everything he needed for his flat. God had given him all brand-new things: white goods, bed, wardrobes, bedding, chest-of-drawers, tables, carpets, curtains - everything he would need to begin his new life. God did all this within a week of him having these needs. God had given him a miracle.

My brother had always done things for others, and now God was blessing him. We truly do have one amazing and awesome God who truly takes care of His loved ones. Amazing!

My brother moved into his new flat at the beginning of September 2018 and all our prayers were answered for him.

I was talking to my prayer friend who knew my brother, and told her what had happened to him. She said to me, "Avril, I want to help your brother. I remember when you helped me, now I am in a position whereby I can help him. I want to give your brother a gift to help him."

She generously gave my brother a gift of £10,000. When he received the gift, he burst into tears. My brother could not believe the generosity of people who wanted to help him, and gave to him the things that he needed to help him get his flat together. He usually was the one who gave to others to help them in their needs.

God was the One who was now taking care of my brother with His people who loved and cared for him. It was my brother's turn to receive the blessings God wanted to give to him. God really did take care of my brother's needs.

He gave God all the glory, honour, praise and adoration and love for all of His faithfulness to him. He would never forget all God had done for him through the heart and core of His people.

Chapter 39

Benalmadena

Psalm 4:8 NIV In peace I will lie down and sleep for You alone Lord, make me dwell in safety.

My husband had booked a holiday for us in Benalmadena, in the Costa-Del-Sol in July 2017. He had also booked a week's holiday in Portugal for our 'Ruby Wedding Anniversary.' He had arranged it all - taxis, hotels and flights.

Now the time had come for us to enjoy our first holiday in Benalmadena. We had been looking forward to spending time together. On the morning we were flying out, we were up early - leaving in plenty of time to park our car at Gatwick Airport. As we were travelling to the airport, we did not realise there were hold-ups due to a fatality on the M25. We were right in the middle of the accident, and held up for a number of hours. We missed our flight to Benalmadena.

I was praying for everything at that time, especially for the people who had died in the accident and for their families. I prayed also if God wanted us to go on holiday, then He would provide another flight for us to catch.

We arrived at the airport and went straight to the desk whose company were flying us to Benalmadena. We told them we missed our flight due to the accident on M25.

The girl on the desk was very sympathetic towards us and she said, "We have the last two seats available on the afternoon flight to Costa-Del-Sol."

We paid for the flights and would be flying to our holiday destination in the afternoon. We would arrive late at our hotel but at least we could go on holiday. Once again God in His faithfulness to me had answered my prayer.

The hotel staff understood the reason why we were late in checking into the hotel. They took us to our room where they had left us a bottle of champagne on ice and a beautiful basket of goodies. My husband and I were absolutely exhausted from the day, but at least we had made it to our destination. We felt totally blessed.

The next day we both felt refreshed and restored, we got dressed and went down to breakfast. The sun was shining, and the day looked bright. We got our sun loungers ready for us to relax in and began to enjoy our day.

My husband went to the pool for a swim. On his return from the pool he said he could not stay in the pool due to a pain in his chest. When I asked him if he needed to see a doctor, his response was no. He did not always tell me what was going on with himself. So, I thought he was okay and I had to trust what he was telling me was right. However, I did notice whilst we were on holiday he did not go into the pool again.

We had a lovely time in Benalmadena. When the holiday came to an end, we could not wait to get home to pick up our dog from our daughter and son-in-law's house where she had been staying while we were away on holiday.

Our daughter and son-in-law were so pleased to see us. Our precious dog also went crazy as soon as we walked into their home. We gave them the gifts that we had bought for them on holiday. We were chatting to them about our holiday for a while then it was time for us to go home. We put all the dog's things into the car, thanked our daughter and son-in-law for taking care of her and we were on our way home.

Chapter 40

Ruby Wedding

Colossians 3:14 NIV And over all these virtues put on love, which binds them altogether in perfect unity.

My husband had made an appointment to see our doctor on our return from Benalmadena. When the doctor examined my husband, the doctor seemed concerned. He wanted my husband to go into the hospital for some tests.

Bit by bit, the hospital was doing tests to eliminate possible diagnoses of my husband's condition.

In the meantime, the time had come for us to go to Portugal for our ruby wedding anniversary. Everything had been booked for our special day. This time we had booked a taxi to take us to and from the airport due to what happened when we went on holiday in Spain. We had also a taxi booked when we arrived in Portugal.

The hotel we were staying at was called 'Tivoli Marina', in Vilamoura. It was absolutely spectacular. We had been given the best room in the hotel. It was such an extra blessing. This ruby wedding anniversary was an occasion we would never forget.

The time we spent in Portugal went very quickly, we had no more than arrived when it was time for us to go home. The week we had was wonderful, it was a holiday we would remember for some time.

Now we were boarding our plane, ready to fly home. We landed at Gatwick Airport, and were walking towards the baggage area to reclaim our luggage, when my husband's mobile rang. It was the hospital in Reading. They wanted my husband to attend an angiogram appointment on 13 September 2017. We were pleased that this appointment had come through as my husband had been waiting for the appointment to come through before we went away on holiday.

We had invited friends and family to join our celebrations for our ruby wedding anniversary. We also invited my husband's three children from his previous marriage to attend. When we sent the invitations to his children, they felt it was not right to attend our celebrations due to it not being a celebration of both their parents. We were shocked at his children's reactions but we accepted their decision. We went ahead having the rest of our family and friends celebrate with us at our favourite restaurant.

The restaurant did us proud. Every one of our guests really enjoyed their meal and the evening was full of laughter. We all had such a wonderful time celebrating. We were all reminiscing over the good old times we all had shared together.

On Sunday 10 September 2017, the actual day of our ruby wedding anniversary, we had booked a table at a local pub to take our immediate family out for lunch. We were able to take our cockapoo dog with us to the pub, as it was a dog-friendly pub. We wanted our dog to be a part of our celebration. Everyone enjoyed the time we spent together.

My daughter and son-in-law had a special cake made for our special day. It was absolutely beautiful. My sister, her son and his girlfriend had come from Switzerland to join in with our celebrations. My nephew's girlfriend had also made us a cake and decorated it for us and she brought it all the way from Switzerland for us. The whole weekend was a great success.

God had been so good to us; we really did love one another and had come a long way since the day we first were married. We had a lot of ups and downs within our marriage, but with God's help He showed me how to overcome the difficulties we had faced. I praise and thank God daily, for all His love, faithfulness, grace, and mercy He had shown towards us.

God has taught me that as long as I pray daily for my family, He was responsible for them not me. I have taken my hands off all my situations now, and have learnt to trust God with all my whole heart that He will work out everything in our lives for good. I will always be so grateful and thankful to God for His Son the Lord Jesus Christ, and to the Holy Spirit of God for dwelling and residing within me. God's grace and strength helps me to continue my life in Him and through Him I am able to cope with all the trials I have in life. There is no other God as glorious as Him and no other God I desire to worship other than Him. I willingly submit, surrender, relinquish and yield my life to God in the name of Jesus Christ and in the supernatural power of the Holy Spirit of God. I have made the decision to walk in complete submission and obedience to the Lord Jesus Christ.

I know before I had a relationship with Jesus Christ, my life in the world was a total mess. God has now transformed my life and I am a new creation, created in Christ Jesus unto good works which God has before ordained I should walk in Him. I am totally grateful to Him for this. He has shown me what true love is: He died on the Cross for me a sinner, and He took the punishment that I should have had upon Himself, so that my sins could be forgiven. He has set me free to love, honour, obey, and trust Him through the Cross and in His Shed Blood has washed, purified, and set me free once and for all. He has pronounced me not guilty. I have given Him my life, to use me where He wills and chooses.

Chapter 41

Gone Before Us

Deuteronomy 1:30 NIV The Lord your God, who is going before you, will fight for you, as He did for you in Egypt, before your very eyes.

The appointment at the hospital had come through for my husband to attend a CT angiogram test. I had been praying about my husband's situation for some time.

God had kept my husband while we were having our celebrations and now he could have his test to find out what was wrong with him.

We had arrived at the hospital on time, but as usual parking our car was difficult. My husband went ahead of me to his appointment, and I would follow him in as soon as I was able to park the car.

It was an absolute nightmare parking the car in the Reading Hospital car park. I kept going round and round in circles hoping someone would leave a space for me to park in. Drivers were becoming impatient and when I eventually did find a parking space it was very tight to get our car in. It did not help when impatient drivers kept beeping their horns at me.

What happened next I could have done without. I parked the car too close to the barrier and I felt I had scraped the car, causing damage. This was another added pressure I had to deal with. I kept crying out to God to help me. I could do nothing about what had happened now. The last thing I wanted was to upset my husband before he went into the department to have his test.

I arrived at the department, the first words my husband said to me was: "You've scratched the car haven't you?" Of course I had to be truthful and tell him I had. I proceeded to tell him what had happened, and he took the news very well.

I sat with him for a few minutes, then he was called in to have his test. Doing the CT angiogram they found it difficult to find a vein in his arm. They eventually managed to get the needle into the vein, but it took the team a couple of times to do the procedure. He had his test, and it was over. Now we could go home. We went back to the car, where my husband looked at the damage I had done.

We got home and our dog was so pleased to see us. We had only been at home a few minutes when the phone rang… it was the hospital. The hospital told my husband to come straight back into the hospital, and on no uncertain terms was he to drive the car in case he keeled over at the wheel. They proceeded to say a medical team would be waiting for him to arrive at the Emergency Department.

He collected the things he needed to take to hospital. Whilst he was doing this, I phoned our daughter to tell her what was happening. My daughter and her husband said they would get a few things together and then they would leave Southampton and come straight to us. They were going to take care of the dog until I knew what was happening. In the meantime, I would keep them informed about what was happening at the hospital. They were both such a support to me.

On the way to the hospital, I kept bringing everything to the Lord in prayer. I knew God would prepare the way for us to go. He would have everything ready for us when we arrived at the hospital. I prayed protection over my husband, daughter, son-in-law and me. I had that assurance the Lord was watching over us. My prayers always sustained me and no matter what my circumstances were, my faith in God carried me through.

We kept our daughter updated of the progress we were making at the hospital. We had the diagnoses; my husband had two pulmonary embolisms on his lungs.

The hospital was now giving my husband the medication he needed to disperse the clots. My husband had to stay in the hospital, and they settled him onto a ward.

Once I knew he was okay, my husband told me to go home. So, I left him in the capable hands of the nursing staff and told him I would be back at the hospital to visit him the next day.

When I got home it was very late. I told my daughter and her husband the diagnosis they found. I had not eaten all day, but I was too exhausted to eat anything as it was very late.

My daughter told me she would walk the dog in the morning so I could rest. I thanked her for this. At least I did not have to worry about the dog. We said our goodnights to one another, and we all went to bed.

I did not sleep well that night. I kept waking up and praying for my husband. Intercessory prayer was my life. I knew God was with me and my family. He had promised me He would never leave me or forsake me, and I knew He would keep His promise to me.

I believed God had saved my husband's life. This all began when we were holidaying in Benalmadena, in Spain. It was amazing that we had our ruby wedding anniversary in Portugal. God had allowed us to celebrate our ruby wedding anniversary with the people we loved, our family and friends. Anything could have happened to my husband whilst we were away, but God had kept us. God in His faithfulness had kept my husband safe in the shadow of His wings. He protected him and rescued him from the evil forces of the earth. I am assured and certain the prayers I petitioned to God for my husband and family, on their behalf have been answered. He is such a loving and faithful God to me. He is always there, ready to help me in His grace, mercy, and peace in the precious name of Jesus Christ, and in the supernatural power of the Holy Spirit of God. He has a plan for each of their lives and no man can put asunder what God has ordained for them.

My daughter, her husband and I went into the hospital the next day. The doctors updated us about my husband's progress. My son-in-law was a paramedic, so the doctors explained to him what had happened to my husband. Our son-in-law relayed the diagnosis to us in a way we could understand. He told me that my husband had two problems going on at once. The hospital thought the pain in my husband's chest was blood clots on his lungs. They were also going to refer him to a respiratory clinic to make sure everything was in working order. The gave him anticoagulants to thin his blood. The hospital was continuing to do tests on him to make sure the blood clots had dissolved with the medication they had prescribed. My husband had a narrow escape. God had kept him through the whole ordeal, and He was taking care of him now.

The hospital had prescribed the right drugs to stop blood clots, he would be on these drugs for the rest of his life. The intermediate artery lesions had to be checked out to make sure there weren't any blockages. Thank God, when the hospital did all the tests they were all clear, so my husband did not need to have a stent fitted.

God did go before us and He did prepare the way. He did watch over us and He did take care of us in our needs as He said and promised. I will always be grateful and thankful to God for all of His love, grace, mercy, and all that He does for us as a family.

Chapter 42

Leave the Land

Genesis 12:1-4 NLT God had told Abram, "Leave your own country behind you, and your own people, and go to the land I will guide you to. If you do, I will cause you to become the father of a great nation. I will bless you and make your name famous, and you will be a blessing to many others. I will bless those who bless you and curse those who curse you; and the entire world will be blessed because of you. So, Abram departed as the Lord had instructed him, and Lot went too; Abram was seventy-five years old at that time.

My husband and I went to have a look at a development area in Chard, Somerset, where they were building brand-new chalet bungalows. My husband and I thought we would like to have a look at the development to see if we liked the area where the development was. So, we booked an appointment with the developer and went to have a look. We loved the showhouse bungalow and we thought it may be right for us. We discussed it and decided we would put our property onto the market as soon as we could.

We got three estate agents in to value our house. The estimates came back and after much prayer, we chose the estate agent we felt was right for us. All we had to do now was sell our property.

Everything was in place when we hit our first obstacle; Brexit. We did not feel it was the right time to sell our house as we did not know how it would work out with Brexit. So, we took our house off the market and let the chalet bungalow go for now. We had put our names down with the developer for a plot for a bungalow, but as yet the bungalow was yet to be built.

I did believe God wanted us to move and I did not want to walk in disobedience to Him. So, I again waited for the Holy Spirit of God, to prompt me to put our house on the market once again.

We waited until Brexit was over. Then, we began looking for properties once again, and this time we were led to Sidmouth in Devon. We had seen a number of bungalows we liked on the Internet, and decided we would go to Sidmouth for the day and have a look at the area.

When visiting Sidmouth, we loved the location and thought we would like to live there. We stopped to have a break and went into an ice-cream parlour. I was waiting for my husband to get our order, when friends we'd known when we lived in Basingstoke saw us, and immediately came over to our table and began chatting. They told me that they now lived in Wellington, in Somerset. They told me they loved the pace of life they were now living and had come to Sidmouth with their daughter and granddaughter for a day out. It was a great surprise for us of all. We told them that we were thinking of moving to Sidmouth, but we had to sell our house first. When it was time for us to leave, we exchanged telephone numbers and promised to keep in touch with one another.

We went to the estate agents in Sidmouth, and put our names down on their lists, so that if any bungalows came onto the market, they would notify us.

Once again, we had to put our house onto the market. We found the estate agent we wanted to sell our house with, and left it to them to sell our home. We had a number of viewings when an offer came in. We accepted the offer after negotiating a fair price. Our house was now under offer.

Then we were hit again, this time with the Covid-19 virus. We were finding it difficult to view properties because of this. We had made an appointment to view two properties. One in Taunton, and one in Crewkerne, in Somerset. We made arrangements with the estate agents to view the properties.

We attended the first appointment in the morning in Taunton. We kept to the rules and regulations because of Covid-19. We arrived for our first viewing, but even just looking at the property from the outside, it looked so uninviting. I did not want to go inside. My husband was insistent, after coming all the way from Burghfield Common he wanted us to go inside. So, under some duress I went inside the property to please him.

It was exactly what I thought. There was no way I could live in a property like this. It would cost an arm and a leg to get this bungalow the way we would want it to be, so we declined the property and told the estate agent we were not interested.

We left the property, and travelled to Crewkerne. We thought we would find the location for the next viewing, and go for lunch in Crewkerne town. We liked the area where the bungalow was situated, but we would have to wait until we viewed the property inside. We had our meal and then it was time to leave for us to view the property.

We got to the bungalow just on time. The estate agent was waiting for us, we got out of the car and went to greet him. He took us into the bungalow, and we were really surprised at what we were seeing. It had everything we could possibly want. My husband would not have to do major works to the property, and everything we saw was good. Yes, we would make changes and have the property the way we would want it to be but at least it was clean and well presented.

After we had finished our viewing, we were chatting with the estate agent and he told us someone else was interested in the property as well. This helped us to make up our minds quickly. We put an offer in straight away, giving the vendor the full asking price and asked the estate agent to ask the vendor not to allow any more viewings to take place on the property.

We had to wait and see whether our offer was accepted or not. What a contrast from the first property we had viewed in the morning. I just felt God had led me to the promised land. I had wait to see if this was the place where God wanted us to be. If so, He would make all things possible. After viewing the property, we went to the market town in Crewkerne to have a look around and to get a feel for the place. We liked what we had seen. In the middle of this the estate agent for the property rang us up and told us the Vendor had accepted the offer, provided we got everything on the move.

We had a coffee in Costa, and rang our estate agent and solicitor, and told them we had found somewhere to live, and we asked them to get the ball rolling to purchase the property for us. Now everything could move forward. Our estate agents updated our buyers, and we could go ahead with the sale.

We did everything our buyer asked us to do, but they were deliberately stalling on the sale. After some deliberation, we decided we would not sell our property to them. It was as if they were playing around with us, so we thought the best thing we could do was pull out of the deal with them and put the house back onto the market, which we did. We informed our vendors about what had happened. In the meantime, I was praying about our situation.

Once we told our estate agent what we were going to do, they agreed with us it was the right thing to do. They felt the same way about what our buyers were doing. So, we instructed them to put the house onto the market once again. Our estate agents told us they had a lot of interest in our property. Not only that, but the government also brought in stamp-duty relief, so we had a certain time to get everything into order.

Within a few days, we had an offer for our house. The vendor in Crewkerne was really pleased about this, and once again it was all systems go. When they knew our house sale had fallen through, they waited for a week, then decided they would put their house back onto the market. We understood them doing this. But whilst they did this, our house came under offer again.

We got our estate agent to get in touch with the estate agent in Crewkerne and told them our position. They told the vendor, and our purchase was back on. We had already most of the paperwork done now, we just had to wait for our new buyers to get their paperwork together.

Prayer sustained me through this time. I knew God would take care of us and He would make all things possible for us. I trusted His Word to me and did not give up. He had the final say over the sale of our house and the one we were buying.

Chapter 43

Emergency

Psalm 32:8 TLB I will instruct you (says the Lord) and guide you along the best pathway for your life: I will advise and watch your progress.

We were now into March 2021. We were still waiting for our house to come to completion. It was Saturday 20 March, and I was waiting for the doctor to phone me as he wanted me to have a consultation with him. I was having my daily shower when I noticed a lump at the back of my right leg. I was troubled by this as it was the leg I had the injury on previously many years ago.

When the doctor phoned me for my consultation, I told him about the problem I had found. He asked me various questions and I answered him to the best of my knowledge and ability. He wanted me to do a few tests at home which I did for him because I had the instruments to do this. After he had finished asking me questions, he told me he wanted me to go to Accident & Emergency. He would inform the hospital that I was on my way.

I could not believe what was happening to me. My husband had to take me to the hospital. Because of Covid-19 he would not be allowed to stay with me at the hospital. I gave the receptionist my details and said goodbye to my husband. I told him I would let him know what was happening as soon as I found out.

I sat down in the waiting area waiting for my name to be called. My doctor had notified the hospital about me. My name was called, and I went through to the cubicle where the house doctor on duty was waiting to speak to me. I went through everything that had happened with him.

He said to me, "Mrs. English, do not worry. We are going to get to the bottom of what is causing this."

I liked the doctor and felt confident in him. He was going to speak to his boss about my case as he wanted to get his opinion on it. So, it was a waiting game. I was having palpitations and did not feel right at all. His boss came and examined me and found I had a faint pulse. They wanted to do further tests on me, so they put me into a short stay ward.

The consultants came and examined me and told me that I would be transferred onto another ward where I would have to stay in hospital. This was the Clinical Summary of what happened next:

Chapter 44
Clinical Summary

Presented after experiencing pain in back of right knee, followed by chest pain and slight shortness of breath. Nothing obvious noted on investigations, although CT scan of chest picked up a possible breast lesion (lump). Referred to breast team via 2ww (2 week wait) pathway. This is a fast-track pathway designed to get you seen quickly.

Also discussed with Cardiology (heart-related issues) team whose impression was that changes that were seen on the Echo (ultrasound of the heart) were NOT worrying given normal levels of blood test and normal ECG (electric heart tracing).

Investigations and Results

• Blood tests:

o D-dimer elevated – this suggests a higher-than-normal level of a chemical that is released after a blood clot is broken down.

o Trops static – this says that your Troponin (a chemical in your body) levels are not increasing, suggesting that your heart muscle hasn't suffered damage and that you haven't had a heart attack.

• CXR NAD

o Chest X-ray – No abnormalities detected.

• ECHO

o Normal left ventricle size, with mild basal septal bulge. This is saying that there is a slight bulge to the structure that divides the two big chambers of your heart. However, it seems that this is not uncommon in elderly patients and can be an indication of high blood pressure.

o As a result, there are sections of your heart wall that are hypokinetic. This means that they have a decreased movement, or don't move as much as you'd expect them to.

o The estimated impact of this is that your Left Ventricle (the chamber that pumps blood around your body) is only emptying about 50-55% of the blood contained within it every time it pumps.

o The Right ventricle (the chamber that pumps blood around your lungs) is a normal size and behaving as expected.

o Both atria (the top two smaller chambers of your heart) both appear normal with no valve lesions seen.

- USS doppler

o This is an ultrasound that is used to check for a clot in your leg. No clot was found where they scanned, which was above the knee of your right leg.

- CTPA

o This is a CT scan of your chest, looking at the lungs. No PEs (pulmonary embolisms – clots in the lungs) were found.

o However, they did note a potential lesion (lump) in the left breast, on the outside edge towards the bottom of the breast.

Plan and Requested Actions

- Started on bisoprolol for blood pressure and atorvastatin for high cholesterol.

- Outpatient CT scan of your chest requested, this time looking at your heart. Also requested follow-up with Cardiology team.

- 2WW follow up with breast team (as noted above).

Bisoprolol

Bisoprolol is a medicine used to treat high blood pressure (hypertension) and heart failure. If you have high blood pressure, taking bisoprolol helps prevent future heart disease, heart attacks and strokes. Bisoprolol is also used to prevent chest pain caused by angina.

Thickened breast tissue with a soft tissue lesion. We need to make sure this is not a recurrence of the cancer.

No blood clot in the lungs.

We are also scanning the leg to make sure there is no clot in the leg.

End of Clinical Summary

The consultants on the ward I was on sent me to have a CT scan. They wanted to check things out with me. When the CT scan was completed, the consultant came to my ward and he gave me the results of what they had found on the scan. I had a mass on the left breast where I had cancer previously. They wanted me to have a mammogram as soon as possible.

The consultant made an arrangement for an appointment to be made for me to have this procedure done. The appointment came through. I was to attend the breast clinic on the 31 March 2021.

The day came, and I was waiting to see the breast clinic nurse. What a surprise I had when I went into the room to see the nurse. Who should be sitting at the desk opposite me but my friend who had taken care of me when I had cancer previously.

She told me I was going to have a mammogram, and if this was clear then I would not have to come back to see her for an ultrasound test.

Well, they did the mammogram, and then I was sent to ultrasound where they did the test and also did a biopsy straightaway. They referred me back to the breast clinic. My friend was waiting for me to give me the results of the tests. I knew in my heart things were not looking good for me but was praying all the way through the tests.

When I went back to see my breast clinic nurse she gave me the news. I had cancer again. Because I'd had already had radiotherapy, they would not be able do that procedure again. She told me I would have to have a mastectomy, but I would have time to think about what I wanted to do before I saw the consultant. In one way I was pleased she was the one who gave me this news. I knew she knew my history, and she would tell me the truth. She was referring me to see the surgeon.

The appointment had been made and I would see the surgeon on 25 March 2021. The news was not good. The surgeon confirmed that I would have to have a mastectomy, because I'd had radiotherapy previously when I had breast cancer before. They could not give me radiotherapy treatment anymore. I had no options but to have a mastectomy operation. He continued to explain to me my options. He told me that he would not be doing the surgery due to his upcoming retirement, but he would get one of his colleagues to do the surgery for me.

In the meantime, I had to have my Covid-19 injection. Then an appointment came through on 15 April 2021 for me to have a CT body scan. I had this procedure done. Then I had an appointment on the 26 April 2021 for a CTA scan. This also was done. On 27 April 2021 I had to have a Covid test. After this test was done, I had to attend the North Block Cancer Centre to meet the surgeon who was going to do surgery on me on the 30

April 2021. She wanted to meet me first before the surgery went ahead. She was lovely, and this was the first time in all the years I been in hospital a woman surgeon would be doing an operation on me.

It was April 30, 2021, I was admitted onto the ward where my surgery was taking place. I was told that I would be first on the surgeon's list. At least I would get it over and done with and I didn't have to wait around. The hospital was aware of the heart problem I had and told me not to worry as they had everything under control. I was waiting to be taken into theatre. The operation was done, and I was in the recovery room where I had a wonderful nurse taking care of me giving me the medication I needed to help me with the pain.

I went up onto the ward in the afternoon where I was given a cup of tea and some toast as I had nothing to eat from the night before. I was put onto a ward with three other patients. I was hoping to be released from hospital the next day, provided everything was okay. The nursing staff was really good to me at the Royal Berkshire Hospital, and I was pleased with the care they had given to me. I was released from hospital the next day. At least I could recover at home in the comfort of my own bed.

The sale of our home was continuing on. We had so much stress over this sale that we would be glad when it was all completed. I had to concentrate on getting over my operation. I was pleased I was able to have the operation before we moved as the Reading Hospital had all my previous notes, so this made my life a little bit easier.

I had a follow-up appointment with my surgeon on 11 May 2021. We had left home early to attend the appointment, but getting a parking space at the hospital was hard as usual. My husband dropped me off and I went ahead to attend my appointment hoping my husband would be able to park the car and attend the appointment with me.

Unfortunately, my husband did not make my appointment as I was called into the surgeon's room. She told me the procedure she had done had gone well. My wounds had healed well. She had found cancer in the lymph node, and she had prescribed Anastrozole to be taken daily for the next ten years of my life. She wished me well with our move and told me that she would forward my notes to the new hospital where I would attend.

A little while later, our solicitor phoned to tell us the exchange would take place on the 24 May 2021, and completion on the 10 June 2021. I had made an appointment with the Prosthetic Nurse so I could be fitted with the right type of bra. This was taking place on 3 June 2021. Everything seemed to be moving forward. We arranged for our removal van to come and pack our furniture up 9-10 June 2021, and they would deliver our furniture on 11 June 2021 to our bungalow in Crewkerne in Somerset.

My husband had booked us into a hotel. 'The Kings Arms Inn' at Montacute, Yeovil. We had the best room in the hotel, but it was a disaster. The shower leaked and there were pools of water all over the floor. I nearly went head over heels because I slipped on the floor of the shower. My husband then had a shower, when he got out of the shower he slipped and said it was like a skating rink because of all the water on the floor.

We got into bed - it was like a trampoline, every time one of us moved the bed bounced up and down. The window kept banging all night long with the church clock chiming on the hour all night long. We did have a laugh at what was happening, but we would not recommend this hotel to anyone else.

We arrived at our bungalow the next day and the removal van was on its way. They arrived and we began unpacking our furniture.

Chapter 45

Settling Down

Genesis 12:1 TLB "Leave your own country behind you and your own people, and go to the land I will guide you to."

We were settling into our bungalow and we were enjoying the area we were living in. We fitted our current furniture into the most suitable places in our bungalow.

The first task we had to do was get a local plumber in to change the WC pans as they were too low to sit on. We then fitted the bedrooms out with new carpets and curtains, changed the doors to give the bungalow a more pleasing look. We ordered new horizontal venetian blinds for all of the windows including the sunroom and chose new furniture.

A while later, we changed the Everhot Range Cooker as it was permanently switched on, therefore expensive to run, and I could not cope with the heat. If we did turn it off it would then take three hours to heat it up again to make a meal. So, we replaced it with a 'Belling Range Cooker' which we had full control over. It left us with no heating in the kitchen though, so we had a new radiator fitted. After a while we replaced the slim line dishwasher with a full-size dishwasher after adjusting the sink to accommodate the extra width of the dishwasher. We were pleased with how the bungalow looked after decorating it and freshening it up. This was all done within one year.

I was enjoying my new life in Somerset. I walked the dog early in the morning and met up regularly with my new dog-walking friends.

In March 2023 I was getting ready to go to bed when I began to feel unwell. My husband had to call 111 and speak to someone in the ambulance service. After they asked him many questions about my symptoms, they told him the paramedics would be out to see me soon.

The paramedics arrived and they began to examine me. After they had finished their examination, they told my husband that they thought I should be taken to Yeovil District Hospital. My husband packed an overnight bag for me to take to the hospital in case they kept me in. My neighbour across the road came across to us after seeing the ambulance outside our home, she offered to take care of the dog until my family came from Southampton.

I arrived at the hospital in the early hours of the morning and the paramedics left me with the medical staff at A&E. They waited for the staff to come and attend to me, then they went on their way to their next patient.

My husband arrived at the hospital not long after the ambulance got me there. The doctors and nurses who took care of me were doing blood tests and various other tests to try to find out what was wrong with me. After doing this they told my husband and I that they were going to admit me into hospital to do further tests.

My husband waited for them to take me onto a ward then he left, saying he would be in the hospital the next day.

They put me into a side room. Then when a bed became available on the surgical ward, they transferred me there. It wasn't long before another patient joined me. We got on really well together which I was pleased about as it made time spending in hospital easier to cope with.

After having a number of tests, finally I got a diagnosis, and they told me I had Ischaemic Colitis. I was discharged from hospital and told they would see me in clinic in three months' time.

Life continued on. I was feeling a bit better, but it didn't last for long. In July 2023, I had walked the dog in the morning, done the housework and watched bit of telly in the evening, then I went off to get ready for bed. I felt a bit nauseous but thought nothing of it. I was on the loo when I felt the sickness come on. I shouted out to my husband to get me our sick bowl, as soon as he brought it, I began to be sick and had no control over the sickness. In the midst of being sick I had a terrible pain in my chest. I told my husband and immediately he dialled, 111. He got through to the ambulance service and they were asking him all questions about my symptoms. My husband answered their questions the best way possible.

After assessing me, they told my husband they would send an ambulance out to me but did not know how long the ambulance would be.

In the meantime, my husband Facetimed my daughter and son-in-law to tell them what was going on with me. My son-in-law had been a paramedic, so he understood, and he began to help my husband. He immediately told my husband to dial 999. My husband took his advice and did what he had asked. After my husband made the call, it was all go. As soon as the paramedics arrived, they assessed me, and after examining me told my husband and I they thought that I should go to A&E at Musgrove Hospital in

Taunton. They told my husband to pack me an overnight bag, and whilst he was doing this, they got me onto the ambulance, put a canular into my hand and prepared me for the journey to the hospital.

It took quite a while to get to the hospital but eventually I arrived at A&E at Musgrove Hospital. My husband followed the ambulance to the hospital. My family wanted to come straight away to our home, but my husband told them to hold fire until we knew more of what was happening to me. They had a toddler, so we did not want to get him out of bed. My husband told them he would ring them as soon as we knew more.

The nurse and doctor asked me many questions. I told them what had happened to me at home and then they told me they were going to move me into a side cubicle where they did various tests.

When the doctor came to my bed with the results from the tests, the first thing he told my husband and I was that the blood test had shown I'd had a heart attack.

My husband and I looked at one another shocked. Although the news was not good, we both were relieved at long last we had a diagnosis.

Everything fell into place for me. This made sense of everything I had experienced over the last few years. When I was in hospital in April 2021, the hospital I was under found I had breast cancer once again. They also had found a heart problem as well. At the time the hospital told me they had to deal with the breast cancer first as this was top priority. I had my mastectomy operation on 30 April 2021.

I understood how I had got to this point. It was during this time that we were in the middle of moving to another location. The pressure was piling up on me, and the only thing that kept me together was my prayer life. I prayed over every single circumstance and situation and included God in everything I did. I knew He would not let me down after all He had a plan for my life and nothing on this earth would thwart those plans God had made. I had the confidence and faith to trust Him to be with me every step of the way. I experienced His presence and had confidence and faith to believe He would deliver me through this ordeal. The hospital was aware of the situation I was in so they would help me sort it out.

My walk with God was my sustaining strength as I recovered from the surgery I'd had. Spending daily time with God kept my head above water.

I was praying through each circumstance I had to face, and I acknowledged God in everything I did. My focus was on God completely. I thanked and praised Him for all the help He was giving to me. I knew the work God was doing within me would carry me through all the trials I was facing.

God has been so good to me over the years, He has never let me down. Jesus Christ is my Lord. Saviour and Redeemer and I know first-hand that He is a great and awesome God who keeps the promises He makes to His people. All I had to do was continue to trust Him. In Proverbs 3:4-6 TLB it says, 'If you want favour with both God and man, and a reputation for good judgment and common sense, then trust the Lord completely; don't ever trust yourself. In everything you do, put God first, and He will direct you and crown your efforts with success.' I absolutely trusted God with my life.

The day after my heart attack, my daughter and husband came into the hospital to see me. I gave them an update of what was happening. They had put me onto a ward as they were going to put a small plastic tube into my wrist artery, so they could see if I needed to have a stent put into the artery vein. I was taken into a room to have this procedure done, but the doctor who was in charge of me told me no matter how hard he tried to put the stent into my artery vein it kept prolapsing and unfortunately, he was unable to do the procedure.

I was taken back onto the ward to rest. My husband and daughter stayed for a while longer, then they went home.

They transferred me to a side room on the cardiology ward as soon as one became available. They had to isolate me from the other patients because I had been in Yeovil Hospital, and there had been cases of Covid-19 reported.

My husband, daughter, son-in-law and grandson were on their way to visit me at the hospital the next day. They were staying with my husband to give him the support he needed.

When they arrived at the hospital and came into my room, my grandson was upset seeing me in the hospital bed. He didn't like it and asked his parents to take him home. My son-in-law suggested that he would take him to an activity so my daughter and husband could visit me. We had our visiting time together and told them I would keep them updated on my condition.

I had every test you could think of. At long last, the results of the hospital's investigations showed that I had 20 percent of blood flowing around the left ventricle of my heart when I was admitted into hospital. After a lot of discussion, they thought the reason for the heart attack was the radiotherapy I'd had previously. I'd been in hospital for 12 days when they discharged me under the heart failure team, who was going to look after me now.

All I had to do was get better. The heart failure team kept a close eye on me and adjusted the medication I needed to get me on the right track. It took ten months before I began to feel better. In the meantime (through blood tests I had regularly) the heart failure team found I had iron deficiency anaemia. I had two weeks of iron infusions and now at long last I was on the mend. The breathlessness went, and I began to do more activities. I am able to walk the dog once again and this has made me happy.

I want to thank all the consultants and nurses on Fielding Ward at Musgrove Hospital for all the love and care and attention they gave to me. In every department I had to go to for tests, the staff were brilliant with me. Nothing was too much trouble.

In all the years I have spent in hospitals, Musgrove Hospital was the best hospital I have ever been in for care. They were working all together as a team in each department I visited. I met a lot of people in the hospital. I continue to pray for each of my new friends and bring them before the eternal throne of God daily.

Conclusion

Isaiah 53:5 NIV But he was pierced for our transgressions, he was crushed for our iniquities; the punishment that brought us peace was on him, and by his wounds we are healed.

I can truly witness and testify to the glory of God. I know without a shadow of doubt He is real and living within me. Ever since I made the commitment to Him in the hospital when I was forty years old, God has been nothing but faithful to me. I am what I am today and have become the person I have become because of God.

I have put my whole trust and faith in Him. He has taught me how to trust in the unseen. I may not see God physically, but I know Him through the Holy Spirit of God, as did His prophets before me. He is the living God. He has taught me how to pray, read and understand the Word of God, and he has taught me how to listen to His voice calling my name. I am totally relying upon Him. Having a personal relationship with Jesus Christ, is the best decision I have ever made. He has been so loyal and true to me. Where man has let me down, I can honestly say that He never has.

My life is so much better now. I am at peace and no matter what comes my way I have learnt to include Jesus in my everyday life, and He will help me through all the difficulties I may have had.

Yes, I have had many challenges, but in the challenges I have a Helper to help me overcome the challenges in Christ. No more am I afraid or discouraged. I know the greatness of the power of prayer and when I seek God with my whole heart, I know He will answer me at His appointed time. I am not alone anymore. Through all the trials and tribulations I have had to go through, God has proven His love and faithfulness to me time and time again. I have learnt to lean upon, depend upon, and rely upon God for all my needs. If you make a commitment to God, I know you will never be disappointed in making the decision. Having a personal relationship with Jesus Christ was the best decision I have ever made, and it could make your life so much better too if you make this decision. The choice is yours to make.

God has given me the gift of love, faith, prayer, discernment, wisdom and insight, enabling me to live my life for Him on the earth. I think the greatest knowledge I have found is to know that before I was even born to the earth, I was with Jesus first.

Jesus also was with God the Father before His Father sent Him to the earth for us all. God sent Him as the Saviour of the world, whether you believe it or not it's up to you. Whether you want to find out the truth or not, it's your choice to make.

All I can say is that over the years I have realised all I can do is tell the truth of what has happened to me in my own personal life, and that what He has done for me He also can do for you. It's up to each individual person to make their own decision about whether or not what I am saying is the truth. I am not able to make any decisions for anyone else's life, it is a decision they have to make for themselves.

I can truly say that, although I had to go into Basingstoke Hospital for major surgery, I am grateful to God for sending the person He sent into the hospital to find the person He wanted her to meet which was me. If she hadn't been obedient to God, it may have taken me a lot longer to find the truth of who God truly was and is. My relationship with God is the most important relationship I could ever have. It does not even bear thinking about not having God in the centre of my life, for He truly does exists for me.

My greatest regret is that I had lost the first forty years of my life, not knowing Him personally. However, I am thankful and grateful to God because I can spend the rest the rest of my life with Him. Jesus, has never given up on me even when I did not know Him personally. He has always been faithful and forgiving to me for everything I had done before I knew Him personally. I give Him all the honour, praise, and glory now and forevermore.

God has a plan for each individual person on this earth, the question is whether you want to follow Him and be a true follower of Christ or not. The choice is yours to make. No one has any right to tell you what you should or should not do. The decision is yours alone to make.

It has been so comforting for me to know through all the trials and tribulations I have been through in life, God, has been in the centre of my life and He has been with me and has delivered me through it all. I am not troubled or anxious any longer. I know who is controlling my life and He is with me to the end of life on this earth.

I will go home to the Kingdom of Heaven and be with Him in eternity for the rest of my life. What joy this brings to my heart knowing I will spend my life in eternity with God forevermore. Hallelujah, all the glory, honour and praise I give to God forever more in the precious name of Jesus Christ my Lord. Amen

Acknowledgments

I am really grateful to all the prayer warriors who have prayed for me to get this manuscript completed. Without them the task in writing this manuscript would have been much harder for me to do. There prayers have been greatly appreciated.

I am extremely grateful to Suzi who has edited this book tirelessly. She is a real blessing to me. Although she has a full and busy life with her husband, child and workplace this did not deter her from editing this manuscript for me. I truly appreciate the time, energy, and effort she has put into doing this amazing task for me. Words cannot express how grateful and thankful I am to her.

Also, I want to thank my precious husband for giving me all the support and help I needed when going through my illnesses. Over the years he has always put my needs first before his own. He has taken time out to take me to numerous hospital appointments, visited me daily when I stayed in hospital and kept things at home running smoothly. He did this without any complaints whatsoever. He knows how grateful and thankful I am to him for all the love and support he has given to me over the years.

I also want to thank my daughter, her husband, and grandson for dropping everything to come and support us. They have always been such an amazing team whose encouragement has helped me to not give up but to continue on to help me in my recovery.

Mostly, I want to thank my God through His Son Jesus Christ, and in the supernatural power of the Holy Spirit of God, who have kept me strong and peaceful when going through many trials. He answered my prayers and the prayers of all the faithful people petitioning prayers to Him daily on my behalf.

God is an amazing God. He has filled me with love, faith, courage and strength to trust Him completely. I have learnt no matter what my circumstances may look like on the outside He was always working in me on the inside. He is continually building my faith on the rock and foundation of

Christ, enabling me to trust Him in faith no matter what my circumstances may be. He has shown me He is in complete control of my life and His plans will be fulfilled for my life.

In Jeremiah 29:11-14 NLT His Word says: "For I know the plans I have for you, says the Lord. They are plans for good and not for evil, to give you a future and a hope. In those days when you pray, I will listen. You will find me when you seek Me, if you look for me in earnest."

"Yes," says the Lord, "I will be found by you, and I will end your slavery and restore your fortunes; I will gather you out of the nations where I sent you and bring you back home again to your own land."

Well, I can honestly say, God is fulfilling His promises to me. He has built my faith and has helped me trust Him in faith completely. I am not anxious, worried, or troubled any longer. He has transformed my life into the image of Jesus Christ, and He has delivered me from the darkness I had allowed to come into my life through my ignorance. Through the supernatural power of the Holy Spirit of God, He has enabled and empowered me with His great tools; He has shown me how to fight the darkness – by reading the Bible and reminding myself of the truth, and by praying daily. He helps me to come to the place that He had planned for me to be.

2 Corinthians 10:4-6 NLT I use God's mighty weapons, not those made by men, to knock down the devil's strongholds. These weapons can break down every proud argument against God and every wall that can be built to keep men from finding Him. With these weapons I can capture rebels and bring them back to God to change them into men whose hearts' desire is obedience to Christ. I will use these weapons against every rebel who remains after I have first used them on you yourselves and you surrender to Christ.

www.ingramcontent.com/pod-product-compliance
Lightning Source LLC
Chambersburg PA
CBHW052054070526
44584CB00017B/2181